顶上英语双语分级阅

SAT/ACT/AP
必考美国历史

顾琼雯　编著

中国人民大学出版社
·北京·

图书在版编目（CIP）数据

SAT/ACT/AP 必考美国历史 / 顾琼雯编著.—北京：中国人民大学出版社，2019.6
ISBN 978-7-300-26744-9

Ⅰ.①S…　Ⅱ.①顾…　Ⅲ.①美国–历史–高等学校–入学考试–美国–自学参考资料
Ⅳ.①K712.0

中国版本图书馆 CIP 数据核字（2019）第 028581 号

SAT/ACT/AP 必考美国历史
顾琼雯　编著
SAT/ACT/AP Bikao Meiguo Lishi

出版发行	中国人民大学出版社	
社　　址	北京中关村大街 31 号	邮政编码　100080
电　　话	010-62511242（总编室）	010-62511770（质管部）
	010-82501766（邮购部）	010-62514148（门市部）
	010-62515195（发行公司）	010-62515275（盗版举报）
网　　址	http://www.crup.com.cn	
	http://www.1kao.com.cn（中国 1 考网）	
经　　销	新华书店	
印　　刷	北京玺诚印务有限公司	
规　　格	185 mm × 260 mm　16 开本	版　次　2019 年 6 月第 1 版
印　　张	12.75	印　次　2019 年 6 月第 1 次印刷
字　　数	253 000	定　价　48.00 元

封面无防伪标均为盗版

版权所有　　侵权必究　　印装差错　　负责调换

Histories make men wise; poets witty; the mathematics subtile; natural philosophy deep; moral grave; logic and rhetoric able to contend. Abeunt studia in morse.

———Francis Bacon

引言——历史是"宇宙"之学

"四方上下曰宇，往古来今曰宙"，这是迄今为止中国古籍中与现代"时空"概念最为接近的定义了，也是对"历史"二字的最佳注解。历史学科是一门"宇宙"之学、"时空"之学——时间的广袤无垠赋予这门学科以宇宙的厚重感；空间的浩瀚无际更点缀以灵动。因此历史学科兼具了厚重与灵动，是一门跨越古今中外的趣味之学。

但在从事教育行业的这些年里，我遗憾地了解到，不少学生和家长仍然将历史当作一门死记硬背的学科，视其为极其耗费精力的"洪水猛兽"，完全曲解了历史学科对学识、思维、语言组织方面的高要求，自然也与个中趣味无缘了。但实际上，无论是哪一国、哪一区域、哪一时间段的历史，都是反映学生思维能力的一面明镜。就以本书的主题——美国历史为例，有志于留学的学生一定对 AP U.S. History、SAT Ⅱ U.S. History 等考试不陌生。The College Board（美国大学理事会）将历史学科纳入标准化和能力考试，并不是为了考验莘莘学子的记忆力，而是通过对历史的解读考查学生的思维高度——论学识，是否能用缜密清晰的因果逻辑线串起美国建国 200 余年以来的大事件；论思维，能否跳出框架，用具有军事高度的眼光对世界各国的发展与未来做出比较、分析与预判；论语言组织，能否在有限的时间内，将严密的思维付诸笔端。但在面临与美国历史有关的考试科目时，学子们往往舍本逐末，忽视思维，只顾背诵。

编写此书的目的正在于此：学生不应该仅将美国历史视为一门应试科目，而应该将自己代入历史，融入美国建国 200 余年来的文化土壤，了解从独立战争到今日美国的每一个历史转折点，批判性地去思考美国腾飞历程中每一个决定的合理性，以美国一国为起点与他国文化进行深入对比，最终站在"历史"这一巨人的肩膀上，学着用历史眼光审视今日时事。此书付梓前业已付诸日常教学，实践证明，用以上高标准自我要求的学生，能够逐渐培养自身的批判性思维，通过考试就更不成问题了。

从开始编写此书至付梓前夕，已二年有余。感谢参与编写《SAT/ACT/AP 必考美国历史》的孙佳怡、朱皓辰、许可、沈韵，感谢出版社的编辑们对此书孜孜不倦的审阅、核对。本书得以与广大家长和学子见面，离不开整个团队在这两年间付出的心血。

希望《SAT/ACT/AP 必考美国历史》能够在教学实践中发挥其最大效用。正如培根所言："读史使人明智，读诗使人灵秀，数学使人周密，科学使人深刻，伦理学使人庄重，逻辑修辞使人善辩。凡有所学，皆成性格。"期盼莘莘学子以美国历史的学习为起点，积累更多对西方文化的体会和思考。

顾琼雯
2019年5月于上海

Content

Unit One	The Meeting of Three Peoples	001
Unit Two	Establishment of the Thirteen Colonies	019
Unit Three	The Evolution of Colonial Period	029
Unit Four	American Revolution	037
Unit Five	The Critical Period	045
Unit Six	Political Parties after American Revolution	053
Unit Seven	Market Revolution and Whig Party	071
Unit Eight	Antebellum Culture	077
Unit Nine	Territory Expansion and Section Tension	087
Unit Ten	Civil War and Reconstruction Era	093
Unit Eleven	South and West During Reconstruction	103
Unit Twelve	Gilded Age	111
Unit Thirteen	Cross-Continental Expansion	117
Unit Fourteen	Progressive Movement	129
Unit Fifteen	World War I	135
Unit Sixteen	America after WWI	141
Unit Seventeen	Great Depression and New Deal	151
Unit Eighteen	World War II—From Isolation to Intervention	159
Unit Nineteen	Cold War and Domestic Society	171
Unit Twenty	Modern Politics	189

Unit One

The Meeting of Three Peoples

1488	Bartolomeu Dias (Portugal) sailed around the Cape of Good Hope
1492	Christopher Columbus (Italian, sailing for Spain) arrived in the New World, beginning the era of European colonization of the Americas
1498	Vasco da Gama (Portugal) sailed to India
1517	Martin Luther challenged Roman Catholic beliefs and practices; initiated Protestant Reformation
1521	Spanish forces, led by Hernan Cortes, defeated the Aztec people, led by Moctezuma
	John Calvin broke with the Catholic Church
1532	Spanish forces, led by Francisco Pizarro, defeated the Inca people
1542	Bartolomé de Las Casas wrote *Brief Account of the Devastation of the Indies*
	The repartimiento reforms began to replace the encomienda system
1585	Founding of the "lost" British colony of Roanoke
1588	Defeat of the Spanish Armada by the English navy
1597	Juanillo's Revolt in Florida
1599	Acoma Massacre in New Mexico

Warming Up

1. Do you think the United States, to some degree, has transformed world history?
2. How much do you know about America's pre-history? Can you figure out what's in the picture?

3. Read the letter below and think about these questions: Who do you think most probably wrote the letter? If you were the king or queen, what would you do in response to the letter? What plan would you have to deal with the New World?

Most High and Mighty Sovereigns,

In obedience to your Highnesses' commands, and with submission to superior judgment, I will say whatever occurs to me in reference to the colonization and commerce of the Island of Espanola, and of the other islands, both those already discovered and those that may be discovered hereafter.

In the first place, as regards the Island of Espanola: Inasmuch as the number of colonists who desire to go thither amounts to two thousand, owing to the land being safer and better for farming and trading, and because it will serve as a place to which they can return and from which they can carry on trade with the neighboring islands:

1. That in the said island there shall be founded three or four towns, situated in the most convenient places, and that the settlers who are there be assigned to the

aforesaid places and towns.

2. That for the better and more speedy colonization of the said island, no one shall have liberty to collect gold in it except those who have taken out colonists' papers, and have built houses for their abode, in the town in which they are, that they may live united and in greater safety.

3. That each town shall have its alcalde [Mayor]...and its notary public, as is the use and custom in Castile.

4. That there shall be a church, and parish priests or friars to administer the sacraments, to perform divine worship, and for the conversion of the Indians.

5. That none of the colonists shall go to seek gold without a license from the governor or alcalde of the town where he lives; and that he must first take oath to return to the place whence he sets out, for the purpose of registering faithfully all the gold he may have found, and to return once a month, or once a week, as the time may have been set for him, to render account and show the quantity of said gold; and that this shall be written down by the notary before the alcalde, or, if it seems better, that a friar or priest, deputed for the purpose, shall be also present.

6. That all the gold thus brought in shall be smelted immediately, and stamped with some mark that shall distinguish each town; and that the portion which belongs to your Highnesses shall be weighed, and given and consigned to each alcalde in his own town, and registered by the above-mentioned priest or friar, so that it shall not pass through the hands of only one person, and there shall be no opportunity to conceal the truth.

7. That all gold that may be found without the mark of one of the said towns in the possession of any one who has once registered in accordance with the above order shall be taken as forfeited, and that the accuser shall have one portion of it and your Highnesses the other.

8. That one per centum of all the gold that may be found shall be set aside for building churches and adorning the same, and for the support of the priests or friars belonging to them; and, if it should be thought proper to pay anything to the alcaldes or notaries for their services, or for ensuring the faithful perforce of their duties, that this amount shall be sent to the governor or treasurer who may be appointed there by your Highnesses.

9. As regards the division of the gold, and the share that ought to be reserved for

your Highnesses, this, in my opinion, must be left to the aforesaid governor and treasurer, because it will have to be greater or less according to the quantity of gold that may be found. Or, should it seem preferable, your Highnesses might, for the space of one year, take one half, and the collector the other, and a better arrangement for the division be made afterward.

10. That if the said alcaldes or notaries shall commit or be privy to any fraud, punishment shall be provided, and the same for the colonists who shall not have declared all the gold they have.

11. That in the said island there shall be a treasurer, with a clerk to assist him, who shall receive all the gold belonging to your Highnesses, and the alcaldes and notaries of the towns shall each keep a record of what they deliver to the said treasurer.

12. As, in the eagerness to get gold, every one will wish, naturally, to engage in its search in preference to any other employment, it seems to me that the privilege of going to look for gold ought to be withheld during some portion of each year, that there may be opportunity to have the other business necessary for the island performed.

13. In regard to the discovery of new countries, I think permission should be granted to all that wish to go, and more liberality used in the matter of the fifth, making the tax easier, in some fair way, in order that many may be disposed to go on voyages.

I will now give my opinion about ships going to the said Island of Espanola, and the order that should be maintained; and that is, that the said ships should only be allowed to discharge in one or two ports designated for the purpose, and should register there whatever cargo they bring or unload; and when the time for their departure comes, that they should sail from these same ports, and register all the cargo they take in, that nothing may be concealed.

……

I beg your Highnesses to hold me in your protection; and I remain, praying our Lord God for your Highnesses' lives and the increase of much greater States.

Historical Highlights

Americas Before European Exploration

A wide variety of social, political, and economic structures had developed among the native peoples in North America in the period before the arrival of Europeans. These structures grew, in part, out of the interactions among native peoples and between native peoples and the environment.

Migration

Because the first humans and civilizations got their start in Africa and the Middle East, historians and anthropologists have had to figure out how Native Americans got to the Americas. Many theories exist about how people first got to the Americas. The most commonly held is the Bering Land Bridge Theory. This has been at the forefront for over 50 years. Basically, the idea is that during the last ice age, about 20,000 years ago (or a little less), lower water levels created a frozen bridge of land. The first settlers of the Americas are believed to have come across this land bridge called Beringia.

Once in North America, these early migrants quickly—within 1,000 to 2,000 years—spread throughout the Americas. The first Americans initially displayed striking cultural similarities. A hallmark of the toolkit associated with the Clovis culture is the distinctively shaped, fluted stone spear points, known as the Clovis points. Archaeologists do not agree on whether the widespread presence of these artifacts indicates the proliferation of a single people, or the adoption of a superior technology by diverse population groups. Nevertheless, Clovis people are considered to be the ancestors of most of the indigenous cultures of the Americas. The ubiquity of these arrowheads, which have often been found in proximity to the remains of mammoths, indicates a similar nomadic hunting culture among these disparate Americans.

Adaption and Diversity

Eventually, the Clovis culture was replaced by several more localized regional cultures from the time of the Younger Dryas cold-climate period onward, about 12,000 years ago. The reasons for this are varied. The mammoth—central to Clovis culture—became extinct. In addition, the Ice Age gave way to the vast variety of climates, rainfall levels, temperatures, and wind patterns that characterize the Americas of today. Over time, the peoples of the Americas adapted to the different regions of the Americas, developing a vast variety of cultural patterns.

Regional Variation

Several distinct regional groupings of native people developed in North and Central America. The people of the Great Plains, occupying the grassy areas east of the Rocky Mountains, depended on hunting the bison. The people of the Great Basin, between the Rocky Mountains and the Sierra Nevada Mountains in present-day California, depended on a variety of fish, game, and plants. Eastern woodlands peoples settled along rivers and depended on hunting small game such as deer. About 4,000 years ago, they developed agricultural practices and pottery. Southwestern peoples adapted to the dry climate, which is without abundant natural vegetation, by cultivating corn about 3,500 years ago. Over time these regional variations gave way to the specific tribal groupings that European settlers and explorers encountered.

Tribes of the Southeast

The Southeast cultural group stretched from the Atlantic Ocean to the Trinity River in what is today Texas and from the Gulf of Mexico north as far as points in modern-day Missouri, Kentucky, and West Virginia. The tribes in this group included the Cherokee, Choctaw, Chickasaw, Creek, and Seminole. These are the peoples who would be referred to by whites as "the Five Civilized Tribes." They were given this title because many of them decided to adopt customs of the colonists. They are also the people who later were victims of the forced relocations known as the Trail of Tears.

The Southeastern tribes settled in river valleys. They were first and foremost farmers with hunting and fishing coming in second as their source of sustenance. They lived in various styles of houses. They included thatched roofs and various styles for the sides.

Tribes of the Northeast

The tribes of the Northeast are the tribes that encountered the Pilgrims. Columbus never even touched the shores of what is today the U.S., so these people are completely different from those who were first encountered by the early explorers.

The tribes of the Northeast lived in the territory from the Atlantic shores to the Mississippi Valley and from the Great Lakes to as far south as the Cumberland River in Tennessee. The peoples in this group include the Iroquois and the Algonquin. These tribes relied on each other for a very long time for trade but also spent a great deal of time as warring enemies.

The Northeast tribes cleared forests to plant crops and used the lumber to build homes and make tools. The women of many of these tribes did all of the work with crops, while the men primarily hunted and fished.

An interesting note on the Iroquois social structure is that it was matrilineal. This means when a couple married, the man joined the woman's family. After marriage, the man was no longer considered a part of his birth family. This family structure was not completely unique to the Iroquois, but it certainly would have seemed odd to European settlers.

While historians do not agree on this, it is sometimes suggested that the Iroquois League is quite famous because some people believe that the cooperation among the original colonies was based on the model of the League.

Tribes of the Southwest

The Southwest territory runs from the southern part of present-day Utah and Colorado down through Arizona and New Mexico. This includes parts of Texas, California, and Oklahoma, and continues into Mexico.

Two basic lifestyles developed in the region: farming and nomadic. Agriculture north of Mexico reached its highest level of development in the Southwest. Examples of farming, or agrarian, people include the Hopi, Zuni, and many other tribes. The nomadic groups include tribes such as the Apache, Navajo, and others.

Agrarian tribes like the Hopi and Zuni developed desert farming techniques that did not require irrigation. They relied on the little natural moisture the area does provide by using specific planting techniques and getting the crops in as early in the season as possible. They traditionally grew corn, beans, and squash. For meat, they also farmed turkeys and did some hunting.

Nomadic groups like the Apache were hunters and gatherers. The men hunted deer, rabbits, and other game. The women gathered berries, nuts, corn, and other fruits and vegetables. Being nomads, they moved from place to place in search of resources. Interestingly, most in these groups did not eat fish, although fish were plentiful. The Navajo were actually a farming people, and they lived in permanent dwellings, but they had two homes, called hogans—one in the mountains and one in the desert. Later their lifestyle included herding sheep. After the arrival of horses, both the Apache and the Navajo lifestyle became closely tied to riding horses.

Tribes of the Great Basin

The Great Basin Culture Area includes the high desert regions between the Sierra Nevada and the Rocky Mountains. It is bounded on the north by the Columbia Plateau and on the south by the Colorado Plateau. It includes southern Oregon and Idaho, a small portion of southwestern Montana, western Wyoming, eastern California, all of Nevada and Utah, a portion of northern Arizona, and most of western Colorado. This is an area which is characterized by low rainfall and extremes of temperature. The valleys in the area are 3,000 to 6,000 feet in altitude and are separated by mountain ranges running north and south that are 8,000 to 12,000 feet in elevation. The rivers in this region do not flow into the ocean, but simply disappear into the sand.

The Great Basin is an ecologically sparse environment punctuated by small areas where water, game, and plant life are abundant. Summers can be fiercely hot and the winters bitterly cold. The land is unfavorable for farming and contains little game for food. This is an area which seems inhospitable to human habitation, yet Indian people have lived here for thousands of years. This was the last part of the United States to be explored and settled by the European-Americans.

Great Basin families were primarily nuclear families: that is, they were composed of a man and a woman and their children. At times, there might be other people who were also a part of the household, such as a younger brother, a grandfather, a widowed aunt. Beyond the nuclear family, people were linked by blood relationships, marriage relationships, adoptions, and friendships. These various and extensive linkages gave the nuclear family access to many different resource areas, something that was very important during times of food resource shortage in the home area.

Tribes of the Great Plains

The Great Plains refers to the vast stretch of land in the United States and Canada that stretches from the Mississippi River to the Rocky Mountains. The Plains Indians are the native groups' most commonly stereotyped in images of Indians in American popular culture. The stereotype often involves Plains Indians riding horses, wearing feathered headdresses, and hunting buffalo. In the minds of many Americans who know this stereotype from movies and television shows, this image represents not just Plains Indians, but all American Indians.

The way of life of the Great Plains Indians was dictated by the regional climate, land, natural raw materials, game, fish, birds, plants, nuts, berries and trees. Their subsistence was related to agriculture and hunting. The natural resources and materials available provided the food and the clothing of the Great Plains Indians. The weather and the changing seasons also affected their way of life at different times of the year. Their language, weapons, trading currencies, beliefs, ceremonies and religions were also important elements of their way of life.

The European settlers introduced the horse to North America and the Great Plains Indians became expert horsemen and hunters. The horse enabled them to adopt a nomadic lifestyle following the great herds of animals.

The Age of Exploration and Conquest

European expansion into the New World was fueled by a variety of factors. In time, the impact of conquest and settlement in the New World was felt in the Old World. Expansion in the Americas resulted in increased competition among the nations of Europe as well as the promotion of empire building.

Causes for European Exploration and Conquest

European conquest of the New World was motivated by European nation-states' need to gain increasingly scarce resources, compounded by rivalry between nations. By the 15th and 16th centuries, European resources were depleting. Each nation-state looked aggressively for new land, and explorers discovering new terrain took possession in the name of the sponsoring nation. Discovery of new land was followed by rapid and aggressive attempts at colonization.

Religious Motivations and the Crusades

The impulse for exploration was further fueled by the European imagination. The idea of "America" antedated America's discovery and even Viking exploration. That idea had two parts: one paradisiacal and utopian; the other savage and dangerous. Ancient tales described distant civilizations, usually to the west, where European-like peoples lived simple, virtuous lives without war, famine, disease, or poverty. Such utopian visions were reinforced by religious notions. Early Christian Europeans had inherited from the Jews a powerful prophetic tradition that drew upon apocalyptic biblical texts in the books of *Daniel*, *Isaiah*, and *Revelation*. They connected the Christianization of the world with the second coming of Christ. Such ideas led many Europeans (including Columbus) to believe it was God's plan for Christians to convert pagans wherever they were found.

If secular and religious traditions evoked utopian visions of the New World, they also induced nightmares. The ancients described wonderful civilizations, but barbaric, evil ones as well. Moreover, late medieval Christianity inherited a rich tradition of hatred for non-

Christians derived in part from the Crusaders' struggle to free the Holy Land and from warfare against the Moors.

European encounters with the New World were viewed in light of these preconceived notions. To plunder the New World of its treasures was acceptable because it was populated by pagans. To Christianize the pagans was necessary because it was part of God's plan; to kill them was right because they were Satan's or Antichrist's warriors. As European powers conquered the territories of the New World, they justified wars against Native Americans and the destruction of their cultures as a fulfillment of the European secular and religious vision of the New World.

The Revival of Trade

The most powerful inducement to explore was trade. Marco Polo's famous journey to Cathay signaled Europe's "discovery" of Chinese and Islamic civilizations. The Orient became a magnet to traders, and exotic products and wealth flowed into Europe. Those who benefited most were merchants who sat astride the great overland trade routes, especially the merchants of the Italian city-states of Genoa, Venice, and Florence. The newly unified states of the Atlantic—France, Spain, England, and Portugal—and their ambitious monarchs were envious of the merchants and princes who dominated the land routes to the East. Moreover, in the latter half of the fifteenth century, war between European states and the Ottoman Empire greatly hampered Europe's trade with the Orient. The desire to supplant the trade moguls, especially the Italians, and fear of the Ottoman Empire forced the Atlantic nations to search for a new route to the East.

The Rising of Centralized Power

At the same time, political centralization ended much of the squabbling and fighting among rival noble families and regions that had characterized the Middle Ages. With the decline of the political power and wealth of the Catholic Church, a few rulers gradually solidified their power. Portugal, Spain, France, and England were transformed from small territories into nation-states with centralized authority in the hands of monarchs who were able to direct and finance overseas exploration.

The Protestant Reformation, Catholic Counter-Reformation and Renaissance

The Protestant Reformation and the Catholic Church's response in the Counter-Reformation marked the end of several centuries of gradual erosion of the power of the Catholic church as well as the climax to internal attempts to reform the church. Protestantism emphasized a personal relationship between each individual and God without the need for intercession by the institutional church. In the Renaissance, artists and writers such as Galileo, Machiavelli, and Michelangelo adopted a view of life that stressed humans' ability to change and control the world. Thus, the rise of Protestantism and the Counter-Reformation, along with the Renaissance, helped foster individualism and create a climate favorable to exploration.

Technological Advances

A series of technological developments encouraged exploration. One aspect of the Renaissance was a gradual increase in scientific knowledge and technological change. The compass, the astrolabe, the quadrant, and the hourglass all aided navigation, helping sailors plot direction, determine speed, and assess latitude. Portulanos, detailed maps, also helped navigators. Portugal developed a quick, sturdy sailing ship called the caravel.

Effects of New World Encounters

Within a generation of Columbus's first journey to the New World, Spanish forces wrested control of much of Central and South America from the native peoples. Also, the European nations including Britain, France, Spain and Portugal were competing for power in the New World.

African Slave Trade

The major European slave trade began with Portugal's exploration of the west coast of Africa in search of a trade route to the East. The Atlantic slave trade peaked in the late 18th century, when the largest number of slaves were captured on raiding expeditions into the interior of West Africa. The expansion of European colonial powers to the New World increased the demand for slaves and made the slave trade much more lucrative to many West African powers, leading to the establishment of a number of West African empires that thrived on the slave trade.

Historians have widely debated the nature of the relationship between the African kingdoms and the European traders. Some researchers argue that it was an unequal relationship in which Africans were forced into a colonial trade with the more economically developed Europeans, exchanging raw materials and slaves for manufactured goods, and one that led to Africa being underdeveloped. Other researchers claim the Atlantic slave trade was not as detrimental to various African economies as some historians purport, and that African nations at the time were well-positioned to compete with pre-industrial Europe.

Relationship with Native Peoples

The sixteenth century saw brutal fighting in the Americas as Spain extended its hegemony over much of Central and South America. One of the more brutal episodes of violence between the Spanish conquistadores and native peoples was the defeat of the Mexica people (also known as the Aztecs), led by Moctezuma, by Spanish forces led by Hernan Cortes (1518—1521). The Incas of South America were defeated by Spanish forces led by Francisco Pizarro (1532).

Encomienda System

The word encomienda comes from the Spanish word encomendar, "to entrust." The encomienda system had been used in feudal Spain during the reconquest and had survived in some form ever since. In the Americas, the first encomiendas were handed out by Christopher Columbus in the Caribbean.

At the time, the Spanish conquistadors needed to find a way to rule their new subjects. The encomienda system was put in place in several areas, most importantly in Peru. Under the encomienda system, prominent Spaniards were entrusted with native communities. In exchange for native labor and tribute, the Spanish lord would provide protection and education. In reality, however, the encomienda system was thinly-masked slavery and led to some of the worst horrors of the colonial era.

The "Columbian Exchange"

Columbian Exchange is a term used to explain about the huge culture exchange that happened between the American and Afro-Eurasian hemispheres. This is right from the plants to animals to even the human population and diseases.

The Columbian Exchange was a vital development in ecological history, and this is because of the assembly of the Old World and the New World. The Old World crops comprise of products like barley, rice, wheat, turnips and others. Prior to the arrival of the Europeans onto the American soil, none of these crops were seen or heard. On the other hand, the New World crops, such as manioc, white potatoes, maize and sweet potatoes, had never been seen by the Spanish and other white settlers from Europe. Similarly in America, there was no Old World animal population like the cattle, sheep, horse and goat. The New World only had the likes of fowl, llama, dog and alpaca. However, after the Columbian Exchange took place, the total face of both sides of the world changed.

However, "Old World" diseases had a devastating effect when introduced to Native American populations via European carriers, as the people in the Americas had no natural immunity to the new diseases. Measles caused many deaths. The smallpox epidemics are believed to have caused the largest death tolls among Native Americans, surpassing any wars and far exceeding the comparative loss of life in Europe due to the Black Death. The consensus is that the vast majority of the Native American population died in these epidemics within the first 100—150 years following 1492.

Christopher Columbus

Though funded by Spanish Court, Columbus was an Italian. Everybody remembers that in 1492 Columbus sailed the ocean blue. Most people remember that his discoveries were all islands in the Caribbean. Today, most people know that Columbus already knew the world was round—he was actually looking for a faster, cheaper way to Asia in order to bring back spices and riches. They've also heard, usually, that he was really harsh to the natives he encountered.

Activating

1. Speech

Historians used to believe that the origin of America Continent originated from Europeans' arrival. However, in recent years, some historians argue that Native Americans before Europeans' arrival also have cultural influences on America. The arrival of Europeans opens a new door for America Continent. Give a speech about the influences of prehistory on today's United States.

2. Debate

1) You have been asked to enter the debate raging among historians regarding Native Americans and their relationship with the environment. You can use the various resources to debate the following statement:

   The Prehistoric people living in North America purposely altered their physical surroundings to better suit their needs.

2) Most American history textbooks provide vivid accounts of the brutality of the Spanish conquistadores toward American Indians. That the Spaniards were often cruel to the native peoples of the Americas is not in question; however, recently historians have begun to question the extent of Spanish brutality. The term, "Black Legend," was coined by a

Spanish historian in 1914 to describe the anti-Spanish propaganda written by English, Italian, Dutch, or other European writers. Although English sources, say, from the 1500s onward should not be discounted, it would be prudent for the students to take into account the origin of these sources. English writers might have been trying to demonize Spanish behavior in order to portray British behavior in the New World in a more favorable light. The British portrayed themselves as altruistic, bringing God and civilization to the inhabitants of the New World, while the Spanish were portrayed as greedy and cruel. Of course, the historical record demonstrates that the British committed their share of atrocities in the New World, probably comparable to those committed in New Spain. The controversy provides us with a cautionary lesson: Look carefully at the source of documents as you use them to write about the past. The documents in the document-based question on the Advanced Placement exam clearly indicate their source. Do not ignore this information.

3. Task for Historian

When studying prehistory, historians, archaeologists, anthropologists, and geographers often have to act like *detectives* to solve the mysteries of the past. Instead of reading books, diaries, or speeches from a specific time period, scholars normally are forced to rely upon artefacts to provide information about ancient peoples and cultures especially about prehistory when written language is not available.

Together, as a team, professionals make inferences about artefacts and how these prehistoric objects explain past events and people. The discovery of new artefacts, in addition to advancements in science and technology, often triggers debate, controversy, and at times even the rewriting of history.

Requirement:

Each of you has received a card identifying your profession for the day (archaeologist, anthropologist, geographer, or historian) and by now you should be assembled in teams based on the colors of your cards. Make sure in each team there are four different professions!

Construct 3 questions that someone in your profession might want to know when analyzing a prehistoric artefact. For example, a historian would want to know, "When was this object made?"

Before trying to solve the mysteries, look at each of the artefacts below and answer the 3 questions you decided were relevant to your field of study. Your ultimate goal is to rely on each other's professional opinions, and as a team make inferences based on the evidence to answer the questions listed under each artefact. Be prepared to give a 5—10 minute

The Meeting of Three Peoples — Unit One

oral presentation in order to teach the class about your line of work as an archaeologist, an anthropologist, a geographer, or a historian and to explain how and why your group reached conclusions for each of the Native American artefacts. Note that the mystery of Artefact #1 has been "solved"—use this example as a guide in your detective work.

Artifact 1—Paleo Period	Artifact 2—Probably Archaic Period
Dimensions: Two and one-half inches	Dimensions: Three and one-half inches by six inches.
What is it? Blades or points.	What is it?
What was it used for? Used to hunt large and small game.	What was it used for?
What role did it play in the culture? The blades look like they were crafted and refined suggesting hunting was an important part of the culture.	What role did it play in the culture?
Relationship between object and environment? People made use of their environment by developing weapons to hunt animals.	Relationship between object and environment?
Artifact 3—Woodland Period	Artifact 4—Mississippian Period
No exact dimensions provided.	Dimensions: Two inches by two and three-quarters inches.
What is it?	What is it?
What was it used for?	What was it used for?
What role did it play in the culture?	What role did it play in the culture?
Relationship between object and environment?	Relationship between object and environment?

Exercising

✎ Which part of today's lesson impressed you most? Try reiterating today's lesson with logic.

_____
_____
_____
_____
_____
_____
_____

✎ Why did Europeans set out for adventures in the 15th century? What were their economic, political, religious, or other motivations? Write a complete essay on this topic.

_____
_____
_____
_____
_____
_____
_____
_____
_____

Homework

✎ There is a Disney movie in 1995 called *Pocahontas*. The movie describes the conflicts between Native Americans and European explorers. In the film, the beautiful Native American princess saved her tribe from invasion with wisdom and love. Also, princess fell in love with a British explorer Smith and saved his life from danger. The story sounds cheering and comforting. But is the story real? You have to search for some information. Furthermore, figure out the real relationship between European explorers and Native Americans in history after the geographical discovery.

✎ The early exploration of Spain and Portugal has great impacts on the America Continent. But is there any influence of such exploration on Europe? Read the material below as an inspiration for brainstorming.

"The gold and silver mined with forced labor in Mexico and what is now Bolivia constituted a windfall that could have been used to develop Spanish agriculture, industry, and commerce. It could have helped the country catch up with northwestern Europe's more developed economies…

"But Spain (in the 1500s) was in the grip of a tiny ruling class of royalty, Catholic Church hierarchy, and landed aristocracy. Two to three per cent of the population owned 97 per cent of the land in Castile, Spain's heartland. The great landowners had no incentive to modernize Spain. They just wanted to raise more sheep and sell more wool. The environmental degradation that overgrazing vast numbers of sheep entailed seems to have bothered the ruling class no more than the cutting of forests for timber to build ships and provide charcoal to smelt domestic Spanish silver ore. And so, what if the wool went to Holland to be manufactured into cloth rather than being processed in Spain itself.

"Meanwhile, successes in the New World swelled the Spanish monarchy's ambitions in the Old. The bonanza of bullion from the Americas encouraged Spain's rulers to build up the army into Europe's largest military force, setting off an arms race that forced rivals to multiply their armed forces as well. Spain hired German, Italian, and Irish mercenaries, building and buying a vast fleet of heavily armed ships. Hegemonic wars against the French, Dutch, and English followed…

"The most lasting and far-reaching effect of the increase of money in circulation was to set off a long wave of inflation that spread throughout Western Europe. To be sure, deficit spending on unproductive armies, navies, and wars as well as debasement of coinage by monarchs in search of additional royal revenue contributed to the run-up in prices."

—A. Kent MacDougall, University of California, Berkeley, March 1992

✎ Imagine a scene: (You can choose one)
1) Before Columbus got the financial support from Spanish King and Queen, he had to persuade them in palace to fund him. How could he manage it? Why would the Spanish King and Queen agree?

2) After Columbus ended his first voyage, he came back to Spain with some presents from New World and reported his experiences to King and Queen. What gifts would Columbus bring? How would Columbus report his adventure? Would he propose some plans about the New World?

Prepare a play on either scene. At least three students form a group to respectively act as King, Queen, Christopher Columbus or other characters you think necessary.

Unit Two

Establishment of the Thirteen Colonies

1588	England defeated the Spanish Armada
1607	Jamestown Colony was founded
1609	Henry Hudson explored area that would become New York
1609—1610	"Starving Time" in Virginia
1619	House of Burgesses was established
1620	Founding of Plymouth Colony
	Mayflower Compact was signed
1622	Attack on Jamestown by local Algonquin Indians
1624	New Amsterdam was founded by the Dutch
1630	Founding of Massachusetts Bay Colony
1630—1640	"Great Migration" of Puritans from England to Massachusetts
1636	Founding of Rhode Island Colony
1638	Anne Hutchinson was banned from Massachusetts
1639	The Fundamental Orders of Connecticut was adopted
1649	Act of Religious Toleration was passed in Maryland
1663	Founding of Carolina Colony
1679	New Hampshire Colony separated from Massachusetts
1681	Founding of the Pennsylvania Colony
1729	North Carolina became a royal colony
1732	Founding of Georgia Colony

Throughout the seventeenth century and the first half of the eighteenth century, the major European imperial powers and different groups of American Indians maneuvered and fought for control of the North American continent. Out of these conflicts, native societies experienced dramatic changes and distinctive colonial societies emerged.

England was eager to duplicate the stunning success of the Spanish in the New World. England emerged as the most powerful nation on the global stage after defeating the Spanish Armada in 1588. It then set its sights on North America. England, Spain, Holland, and France all made attempts to establish control over different areas of North America. These efforts led to different patterns of colonization and different types of interactions with American Indian groups.

Warming Up

1. Have you seen documentaries about the establishment of 13 colonies which later became the United States of America? Share your experiences.

2. What cultural changes did the Old World bring to the New World? What do you think is happening in the following pictures? What do you think happened when people established colonies?

Historical Highlights

Under British control, the original thirteen colonies were both strikingly similar in some aspects, and quite different in others.

Similarity of Thirteen Colonies

Mercantilism

Mercantilism is a theory prevalent in Europe during the 17th and 18th centuries asserting that the wealth of a nation depends on its possession of precious metals and therefore that the government of a nation must maximize the foreign trade surplus, and foster national commercial interests, a merchant marine, the establishment of colonies, etc.

Differences of Thirteen Colonies

Due to geographical, cultural and historical reasons, the thirteen colonies went through different patterns of development. Ultimately, their differences had a greater influence on history. These differences were felt through many following generations.

Southern Region
Virginia (1607)

In 1607 Jamestown was the first permanent English colony in America. Jamestown was founded because of the potential for economic success. The colonists came because of gold and adventure.

Famine, disease and conflict with local Native American tribes in the first two years brought Jamestown to the brink of failure before the arrival of a new group of settlers and supplies in 1610. Tobacco became Virginia's first profitable export, and a period of peace followed the marriage of colonist John Rolfe to Pocahontas, the daughter of an Algonquian chief. During the 1620s, Jamestown expanded from the area around the original James Fort into a New Town built to the east; it remained the capital of the Virginia Colony until 1699.

Maryland (1632)

The founder of Maryland was John Calvert, Lord Baltimore. The colonists supported themselves by farms which they grew flax (to make cloth), grains such as corn, wheat, vegetables, tobacco, and fruit trees. Most of the colonists were Catholic.

North and South Carolina (1663)

The North and South Carolina colonies started out as one Carolina Colony and was founded by eight different aristocrats. The eight were given land by King Charles as a gift to thank them for their support. Settlers became sick with malaria from mosquitoes that bred there. The economy was mostly agrarian, and they grew cotton, tobacco, indigo, and rice. Later, the Colony split into what we now know as North Carolina and South Carolina.

Georgia (1732)

Georgia was founded as a haven for poor debtors. The colony included English, Africans, and Native Americans as well as debtors from France, Scotland, Ireland, Wales, Germany, and the Netherlands. The economy in Georgia was based mostly on farming. Cash crops included cotton, indigo, tobacco, and rice. Eventually Africans were used on the plantations. The religion in Georgia was based on religious tolerance and freedom.

Northern Region

Puritans

Puritan was the name given in the 16th century to the more extreme Protestants within the Church of England who thought the English Reformation had not gone far enough in reforming the doctrines and structure of the Catholic church; they wanted to purify their national church by eliminating every shred of Catholic influence. In the 17th century, some Puritans immigrated to the New World, where they sought to found a holy commonwealth in New England. Puritanism remained the dominant cultural force in that area into the 19th century.

Massachusetts

Plymouth was founded by the Pilgrims, a Puritan group fleeing religions persecution, in 1620. The Pilgrims arrived on the Mayflower near Plymouth Rock. Plymouth was made up mostly of English settlers and Native Americans. When the Pilgrims landed they drafted the Mayflower Compact to work for the good of the colony. The Massachusetts Bay Colony was founded in 1630 under the leadership of John Winthrop. The religion in Massachusetts was based on the "purity and conscience of liberty of worship." There was little tolerance for religions other than the Christian religion. There was generally no separation of church and state in areas controlled by the Puritans.

New Hampshire (1629)

The colony was founded for profit from trade and fishing.

Rhode Island (1636)

Roger Williams, a preacher and an original member of Massachusetts Bay Colony, was expelled when he and his followers conflict with other leaders of Massachusetts who were Puritans. A few aristocratic families who settled in Rhode Island owned large farms that were like southern plantations. Rhode Island was founded as a place for religious freedom and was populated by Quakers, Baptists, Anglicans, Puritans, and Congregationalists.

Connecticut (1636)

Connecticut was also founded because Puritans were not allowed to follow their Puritan faith. The people of Connecticut were mainly made up of Native Americans, Europeans, and Dutch. Common food that was raised in the colony was corn, pumpkins, beans, squash, and apples. Many men hunted for game and the women weaved baskets. Since most of the colony was made up of Puritans the colonists followed the Puritan religion. Connecticut had what has been referred to as the world's first democratic constitution. This was called "The Fundamental Orders of Connecticut."

Middle Region

Quakerism

The Quaker movement took shape in the seventeenth century and its foundation as the Society of Friends is associated with George Fox (1624—1691) who was born in Fenny Drayton, Leicestershire, England. Quakerism has evolved as a distinct approach to life founded on a Christian tradition but guided by the inner light of each in a religious organization which has no hierarchy and which does not seek to convert people (proselytize) but rather each applies their principles as a way of life thereby making the practical example of ways and means a spiritual foundation of improving the world and the lot of others. To that extent Quakerism contains a latitude of pragmatism characterized by tolerance as opposed to the more restricted interpretation of many institutionalized religions founded upon faith and an often literal interpretation of scriptures as laws, commands and rules monitored and imposed by ministers and clerics.

New York (New Amsterdam) (1624)

The Colony of New York was founded by the Dutch settlers. They set up trading post, and exploited the area's rich natural resources. The colony was populated by Native American tribes, Dutch settlers, English Puritans, indentured servants, and African slaves. The colony was run by a governor appointed by the King of England. Sometimes the colony was able to gain more freedom, and have some self-governing.

New Jersey (1664)

New Jersey was founded in 1664. Its founders were religious and political freeman. The colony was made up mostly of Dutch, Swedes, and Germans. Their government was known as the "Concessions". It granted religious freedom to English men. The economy was based mainly on farming.

Delaware (1638)

Delaware was founded in 1638 by the Dutch settlers. Most of Delaware's population is Dutch or Swedes. The majority of their religion is Roman Catholic or Jew. Their economy grew with farming and agriculture.

Pennsylvania (1681)

Pennsylvania was claimed for England by John Cabot in 1497. William Penn was given a land grant in 1681. He was a Quaker. Pennsylvania was founded as a colony where people would be allowed to worship as they chose. The colony was made up of English Quakers and other Protestants. Slaves made up about 20 percent of the population. In the colony the religion had a very strong tradition of tolerance and welcomed settlers seeking religious freedom. The colony offered political freedom and self-government. Every free man in the colony elected 200 representatives to the Pennsylvania General Assembly each year. The men voted on laws that were proposed by the Provincial Council, 72 men also elected annually. The Governor oversaw the legislature.

Indentured Servant

Indentured servitude refers to the historical practice of contracting to work for a fixed period of time, typically three to seven years, in exchange for transportation, food, clothing, lodging and other necessities during the term of indenture.

Activating

1. Debate

There are several important historiographical questions surrounding the English settlement of North America. Historians have questioned traditional accounts contrasting English and Spanish colonization. In such accounts, the Spanish are portrayed as brutal, almost to the point of being sadistic, in their treatment of the native populations of Central and South America. Traditional accounts of English settlement of North America have deemphasized warfare with American Indians and focused more on theological issues among the Puritans and the economic development of the colonies. More recently, historians have questioned the veracity of some of the more graphic descriptions of Spanish actions in the Americas, and have shed new light on the history of violence by the English against native peoples.

Another question that has engaged historians is the comparison between the New England and the Chesapeake colonies in the seventeenth century. Historical accounts have looked for differences between the northern and southern regions—examining such differences almost from the first day of settlement. To some degree historians can be faulted for reading the more recent past (the Civil War) into the more distant past (the colonies in the 1600s) and concluding that the bloodshed of the 1860s was rooted in seventeenth-century patterns of development. It is open to interpretation whether the differences between the regions are more important than the commonalities.

2. Debate

Historians have different opinions on mercantilism. Some believe that mercantilism is the origin of capitalism and lays the foundation for America's economic prospect. Others argue that mercantilism puts emphasis on governmental supervision, which does more harm than good. The famous economist Adam Smith once voiced his stand. Find out Adam Smith's viewpoint and have a debate on the subject in two groups.

3. Speech

Imagine you were living in America Continent in the colonial period; which place would you choose to live in? Choose your ideal place and prepare a speech to describe the social conditions.

Exercising

✍ Religion is one of the prominent elements in America's colonial period. Read the following excerpt for inspiration and think about why Puritanism is popular in America and how to comment on Puritanism.

"There is little doubt that Puritanism was closer to medieval theory than the material goals and values of a growing middle class that was becoming prominent in England and western Europe after the fifteenth century. While the Puritan never thought of his religion in economic terms, he did emphasize the fact that man could serve God not by withdrawing from the world, but rather by following an occupation or calling that served the world.

"In spite of the proximity of certain Puritan values to the rising capitalistic ethic, Puritanism was more medieval than modern in its economic theory and practice. The idea of unrestrained economic individualism would have seemed a dangerous notion to any self respecting Puritan. The statute books and court records of seventeenth

Establishment of the Thirteen Colonies — Unit Two

century Massachusetts abound in examples of price and wage controls instituted by the government of the colony. The Puritans, furthermore, always looked upon wealth as a gift from God given in the form of a trust; and they emphasized not only the benefits that accrued from work and wealth, but also their duties and responsibilities. In 1639, for example, one of the richest merchants in the colony was fined by the General Court (the highest legislative body) for excessive profiteering, despite the fact that there was no statute against the practice. The Puritans could never separate religion and business, and they often reiterated the medieval conception of the 'just price.'

"In the long run, however, the Puritan ethic, when divorced from its religious background, did serve to quicken and stimulate the spirit of capitalism. The limitations placed by the Puritans on the individual and the freedom of movement within society were subordinated as the time went on in favor of the enterprising and driving individual who possessed the ability and ambition to rise through his own exertions."

—Gerald N. Grob and Robert N. Beck, *American Ideas*, 1963, p.63

Your thinking:

_____
_____
_____
_____
_____

✎ Compare and contrast the ways in which thirteen colonies in America were established and went through changes. (800—1200 words)

Homework

✎ Imagine you were an adventurer who explored the New World. You had the habit of writing journals every day to record what you had seen and done. Try designing a set of diaries recording your experiences in the New World. You can freely decide the content of journals but it must include the following: your preparation before setting out, a brief introduction of the New World and some personal thinking.

✎ Read several poems about the colonial period. Now suppose you were a great poet at that time. Does every region—North, South and Middle part have different cultural characteristics? You can choose one from all three regions as your residence and write a poem. Your poem should reflect the local spirit as well as be agreeable to hear.

✎ You've read the social conditions of thirteen colonies. Try to draft laws for one specific colony. How to operate the colony as a leader according to the laws?

Unit Three

The Evolution of Colonial Period

1662	Half-Way Covenant
1675—1678	King Philip's War
1676	Bacon's Rebellion
1680	Pueblo Revolt (Pope's Rebellion)
1686	Creation of the Dominion of New England
1688	The Glorious Revolution
1689	New Englanders toppled the Dominion of New England
1692	Salem witch trials
1733	Molasses Act
1735	Zenger trial
1739	Stono Rebellion
1741	Arrests and executions in the supposed "Negro Plot" in New York City Jonathan Edwards' sermon, "Sinners in the Hands of an Angry God"

Warming Up

Can you comment on the development of the three regions of colonies on the basis of establishment of thirteen colonies?

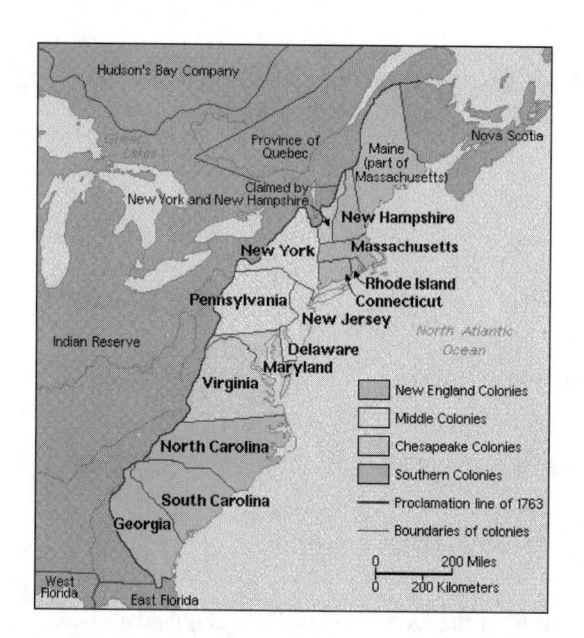

Historical Highlights

Differences in Colonies' Development

Southern Region

The most remarkable feature of the southern colonies is agriculture. Through years, indentured servitude finally developed into slavery system. Such developing pattern predicts the future characteristic of Southern part of the United States.

Bacon's Rebellion

Virginia farmers led by Bacon clashed with both Indians and the colonial government over frontier expansion in 1675. Bacon marched to Jamestown in a revolt with his armed followers. This rebellion ended with Bacon's death in September 1676.

Guiding Question: What caused Bacon's rebellion?

Resistance to Slavery

Although there weren't many outright rebellions, there were lots of attempts occurring in the south. The most famous slave rebellion of the colonial period was the Stono, South Carolina rebellion in 1739. Other mild slave rebellions included working slowly, breaking tools and feigning ignorance.

Northern Region
Decline of Religion

Although the original purpose of building New England colony was for the Puritans to have a home, a decline in religious piety happened later due to death or immigration of first generation.

Half-Way Covenant

A move designed to liberalize membership rules after decline of religion happened. The Half-Way Covenant is a compromising form of membership, which allowed people to be baptized, but prevented them from partaking in Communion or voting on church matters.

King Philip's War

An armed conflict between Native Americans and the New England colonists burst out in 1675 and lasted until about 1678. King Philip, the leader of Native Americans, first attacked the New England colonists after they executed three of King Philip's tribal members for murdering another Native American who had converted to Christianity and believed by King Philip to be a spy for the colonies. However, the Native Americans became overwhelmed after colonists fought back and left the area. This led to a large expansion of colonial territory into formerly Native American lands.

The Dominion of New England

The Dominion of New England was an English governing organization that revoked the charters of all the colonies north of Maryland and united these colonies into a single administrative unit from 1686 to 1689.

Salem Witch Trials

A series of prosecutions of suspected witches who were believed to have the Devil's magic in colony Massachusetts between February 1692 and May 1693. The most notorious accusations occurred in and around Salem, Massachusetts. The authorities there executed 19 suspected witches.

Middle Region

Economy

The Middle Colonies had a free market economy which was beneficial in terms of economic development. Many colonists were farmers who grew crops and raised livestock. Factories also produced many goods including iron, paper and textiles. They traded these goods with other colonies and European countries.

Slavery

Slavery existed in all the colonies of British North America, but it didn't become a central part of the economy in most of northern colonies, although New York had an especially large slave population. Nonetheless, slavery in the north was never stronger than in the south. Northern slaves worked as sailors, domestic servants, longshoremen, and artisans' assistants.

Diversity

The middle colonies had great diversity both in religion and in immigrants. No specific religious belief dominated the middle colonies. Colonists there came from different nations, including the Netherlands, Germany, Sweden, etc.

Similarities in the Colonies' Development

Influences of the Glorious Revolution

James II had been overthrown in England in a coup and the plotters replaced him with King William and Queen Mary. William and Mary collaborated with Parliament and signed the English Bill of Rights which included habeas corpus. This bloodless coup is called the Glorious Revolution in history. This revolution also greatly affected the colonies. This move freed the northern colonies from the control of the Dominion of New England. Additionally, an army lead by John Coode defeated the army of Maryland's colonial government in 1689, which encouraged England to adopt a colonial policy called Salutary Neglect.

Salutary Neglect

Salutary neglect is a British policy in early 1700s which allowed the colonies virtual self-ruling as long as colonies cooperated with British economic policies and supported British during war against France and Spain.

Freedom of the Press

The colonists came to realize the value of a free press. One famous case that set legal precedent at that time was the Zenger Trial, in 1735. John Peter Zenger, a New York newspaper publisher, was arrested and charged with libel for printing articles criticizing the governor. Zenger's lawyer helped him win the trial by proving that what Zenger printed was the truth. After this case, more newspapers were willing to print news freely.

American Enlightenment

The American Enlightenment occurred throughout the eighteenth and nineteenth centuries, during which European thinkers questioned traditional authority and thought that humanity could be improved through rational thought, practical change, and science. Some remarkable and famous thinkers were Rousseau, John Locke, Montesquieu and Voltaire.

The Great Awakening

The Great Awakening was a religious resurgence movement occurring in the British colonies during the mid-eighteenth century. Powerful evangelical preachers traveled throughout the colonies to give emotional sermons that touched listeners deeply. One famous sermon from Jonathan Edwards was "Sinners in the Hands of an Angry God". The Great Awakening aroused the American people's consciousness of human rights and was considered the spiritual premise for the American Revolution.

Activating

1. Debate

Historians continue to debate several important issues in regard to the development of slavery. Historical work has examined the relationship between racism and slavery. Did African slavery develop because of preconceived notions of racial hierarchies, or did these notions of superior and inferior races develop over time to justify the continued enslavement of hundreds of thousands, and finally, millions of Americans?

In addition, historians have debated whether the thirteen colonies' ties to Great Britain were beneficial or not to the colonies. On the one hand, mercantilist rules restricted colonial economic activity. The economic activity that was permitted was designed to benefit Great Britain more than it did the colonies. To support the argument that mercantilist rules hampered colonial economic development, historians have cited many colonists complaining about being "oppressed" and reduced to the status of "slaves." Other historians note that many of the mercantilist rules were simply ignored by the colonists.

2. Speech

Please describe the whole social condition of America's colonial period.

3. Presentation

Imagine you were one of the government officers in Northern or Southern part. You are going to have a meeting about the issues in the society. Express your concern and anticipation, e.g., slavery, church decline…

Exercising

✎ Choose two of the following and analyze their impact on colonial North America's development between 1620 and 1776: Puritanism, the Enlightenment, and the 1st Great Awakening. (500—800 words)

_____

_____
_____
_____
_____
_____
_____
_____
_____
_____

✎ During the 1st Great Awakening, the press achieved a great degree of freedom. Suppose you were one of the greatest journalists at the time. Try writing an **objective** report on the evolution of thirteen colonies and the social trend. (800—1200 words)

_____

_____
_____
_____

The Evolution of Colonial Period — Unit Three

_____
_____
_____
_____
_____
_____
_____
_____

Homework

✎ The Great Awakening endowed colonies a sense of self-consciousness. Read some documents reflecting people's desire for freedom. Now you are going to design a drama. The whole class can be divided into two groups representing southerners and northerners respectively. Combine the real social conditions of America continent in the 18th century. The drama shall mirror the spirit of freedom and defence.

✎ You are going to have a seminar about the drama you made above. Please read the scripts of the dramas from the other groups and discuss the authenticity of the stories. For instance, you might ask whether it is suitable to arrange one specific scene in the drama. Also, you can think about the setting, the theme and the background of the drama. The two groups can discuss with each other.

✎ Slavery took shape during the evolution of thirteen colonies. How about imagining you become one of the slaves in the 17th century? As a slave, you would like to express your feelings or encourage yourself during the work. Please write a song from a slave's perspective. Remember to add your personal thoughts and emotions to the song.

Unit Four

American Revolution

1754	Beginning of French and Indian War
1763	Treaty of Paris ended French and Indian War
	Royal Proclamation of 1763
1764	March of the Paxton Boys
	Sugar Act
	First Committee of Correspondence established in Boston
1765	Stamp Act
	Stamp Act Congress
1766	Declaratory Act
1767	Townshend Acts
1770	Boston Massacre
1772	*Gaspee* Affair
1773	Tea Act and Boston Tea Party
1774	Intolerable (Coercive) Acts
	First Continental Congress

1775	Battles of Lexington and Concord
	Second Continental Congress
1776	Publication of *Common Sense* by Thomas Paine
	Declaration of Independence
1777	Articles of Confederation
	Battles of Saratoga
1778	France entered the war on the side of the colonists
1781	Articles of Confederation was ratified by states
1783	Treaty of Paris ended the American Revolution

Warming Up

1. What do you know about the American Revolution? Have you watched any movies on the topic? Discuss your knowledge and opinions.

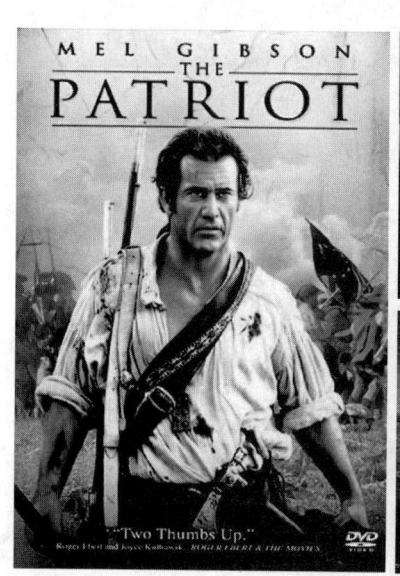

2. Have you ever heard about the American National Anthem? Take a look at the lyrics and exchange your thoughts on the song.

The Star-Spangled Banner

Oh, say! Can you see, by the dawn's early light,
What so proudly we hailed at the twilight's last gleaming?
Whose broad stripes and bright stars, through the perilous fight,
O'er the ramparts we watched were so gallantly streaming?
And the rocket's red glare, the bombs bursting in air,
Gave proof through the night that our flag was still there:
Oh, say! Does that star-spangled banner yet wave
O'er the land of the free and the home of the brave?

On the shore, dimly seen through the mists of the deep,
Where the foe's haughty host in dread silence reposes,
What is that which the breeze, o'er the towering steep,
As it fitfully blows, half conceals, half discloses?
Now it catches the gleam of the morning's first beam,
In fully glory reflected now shines in the stream:
'Tis the star-spangled banner! Oh, long may it wave
O'er the land of the free and the home of the brave!

And where is that band who so vauntingly swore
That the havoc of war and the battle's confusion,
A home and a country should leave us no more?
Their blood has washed out their foul footsteps' pollution!
No refuge could save the hireling and slave
From the terror of flight or the gloom of the grave:
And the star-spangled banner in triumph doth wave
O'er the land of the free and the home of the brave.

Oh, thus be it ever, when freemen shall stand

Between their loved homes and the war's desolation!
Blest with victory and peace, may the heaven-rescued land
Praise the Power that hath made and preserved us a nation!
Then conquer we must, when our cause it is just,
And this be our motto: "In God is our trust."
And the star-spangled banner in triumph shall wave
O'er the land of the free and the home of the brave.

Historical Highlights

French and Indian War

The French and Indian War was a continuous fight between the Great Britain and France, in which both sides fought over territorial expansion.

Fighting

With the stretching of war line, the colonies could not be avoided to get into this long-lasting war. In 1761 French surrendered at Montreal.

The Treaty of Paris (1763)

France gave out its entire North American lands. So Great Britain took over all French territory in Canada, east of the Mississippi River. But the British government shocked the North American even before they had a chance to celebrate. Almost immediately, the British government attempted to handle a serious problem—the war has been fought so long that the debt it accumulated during this time became a burden for the development of the British Empire.

It is important to remember that, before the the end of this war, salutary neglect allowed both Great Britain and the colonies to benefit under generally unenforced mercantilist rules. Believing its victory benefited the colonists, the British asked for a so-called fair return by ending salutary neglect. So, after the war, the British government enacted a series of strict and unreasonable rules that many colonists found objectionable, unleashing a resistance movement that later resulted in the American War for Independence.

American Revolution Unit Four

Royal Proclamation of 1763

The Royal Proclamation of 1763, which drew a line through the Appalachian Mountains, ordered the colonists not to settle beyond the line. The British government did not want to provoke additional warfare with native people in the region. Colonists' need for more lands was ignored.

The Following Acts

Sugar Act (1764)

Main content: raising the tax of buying sugar in the colonies.

Stamp Act (1765)

Main content: adding taxes of purchasing every stamp.

Quartering Acts

Main content: sustaining army in Boston, forcing the local to feed the troops.

Townshend Acts (1767)

Main content: A series of acts named after Charles Townshend, the Chancellor of the Exchequer. The acts imposed additional taxes on the colonists.

The Local Protests

Stamp Act Congress

The Stamp Act Congress is the first and most significant protests against British Stamp policies.

Committees of Correspondence

It is the virtual shadow governments in the colonies, assuming powers and challenging the legitimacy of the legislative assemblies and royal governors in 1770s.

Crowd Actions

Unreasonable acts angered American people and led to numberless Crowd Actions. Sons of Liberty groups occurred, which launched occasional attacks towards Stamp Act agents. And even the home of the lieutenant governor, Thomas Hutchinson, was attacked. The Stamp Act itself was rescinded because of these actions. (1766)

Appearance of Conflicts

The Boston Massacre

A disagreement escalated into a scuffle. Angry colonists heckled and threw stones at British troops. Finally, the British troops opened fire on the colonists, resulting in five deaths.

Gaspee Affair

In 1772, the *Gaspee* Affair represented a shift toward more militant tactics by colonial protestors. A British revenue schooner, the *Gaspee*, ran aground in shallow waters near Warwick, Rhode Island. Local men boarded the ship, looted its contents, and finally torched it.

Tea Act and Boston Tea Party

In 1773, the British passed the Tea Act, which eliminated British tariffs from tea exported to the colonies by the British East India Company. The colonists responded by dumping cases of tea into the Boston Harbour.

Intolerable (Coercive) Acts

The governance of Massachusetts was under direct British control, allowing British authorities to move trial from Massachusetts to Great Britain. The port of Boston was closed. Britain even required Boston residents to house British troops.

The Mental Awakening

Common Sense was a bestselling pamphlet Thomas Paine published in 1175—1776. It suggested that the American colonies should declare independence to Great Britain.

The Declaration of Independence

On July 4, 1776, the delegates to the Second Continental Congress formally ratified the Declaration of Independence. The body of the Declaration of Independence is a list of grievances against George the Third. It also contained key elements of Locke's natural rights theory. These ideas have further influence in the later development of the United States.

Shot Heard Round the World: Lexington and Concord

A fighting began between colonists and British troops in Lexington and Concord in April 1775. The event symbolized a certain shift of colonies' attitudes from resistance to rebellion.

End of the American Revolution

The American Revolution took about six years to have a final conclusion. Starting in the north, this war ended October 1781 as the British Army general Charles Cornwallis surrendered. It took another two years to discuss the Treaty of Paris (1783). This treaty allowed the United States to gain all the land which was once owned by the British Empire.

American Revolution Unit Four

Activating

1. Speech

Suppose you were one of the leaders of the protests against Britain. Give a sensational speech on rallying people to fight against British tyranny. Your speech should contain the following elements: what's the current situation, why there had to be resolute actions and how to tackle the problem.

2. Group Presentation

Form a group of 3—4 students. Imagine such a scene: before American colonies determined to fight against British government, a predictor foresaw American Revolution and told the Parliament of the doomed independence of America. Suppose your group was Parliament and you were all ministers. What would you do? Would you prevent such Revolution or let it go? Why? If you wanted to prevent it, how could you prevent the American Revolution and keep America Continent the British colonies?

Exercising

✍ Imagine you were the military minister of America during War of Independence. There is a mission requiring you to give a military report to the president. You will include analysis of the war from many perspectives, e.g., you could talk about the situation of America, Britain, and the whole world. (500—1000 words)

_____

_____
_____
_____
_____
_____
_____
_____

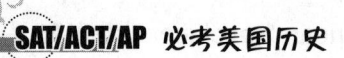

✎ Use a chart to compare and contrast the government system in contemporary America and Britain.

America	Britain

Homework

✎ Please choose a theme covered in this unit and draw a satirical political cartoon to illustrate your theme.

✎ Have a brainstorm about the reasons of the American Revolution. It is recommended to rank the necessities of the reasons with stars. Your results should be like this:

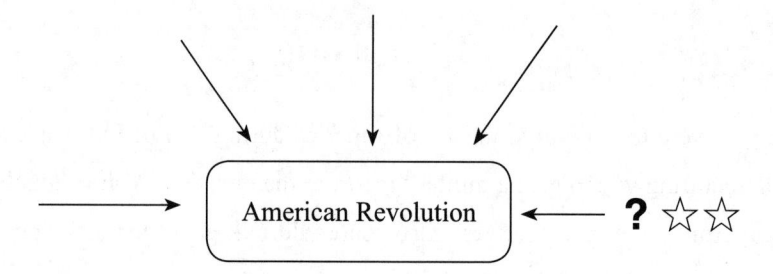

→ American Revolution ← ? ☆☆

✎ Team up! Work as a group to do research on the founding fathers.

Unit Five

The Critical Period

1781	Articles of Confederation was ratified by states
1783	Treaty of Paris ended the American Revolution
1784	First Land Ordinance
	Treaty of Fort Stanwix
1785	Second Land Ordinance
1786	Shays' Rebellion
	Annapolis convention to revise Articles of Confederation
1787	Northwest Ordinance
	Constitutional Convention in Philadelphia
1788	New Hampshire became the ninth state to ratify the Constitution, and it was agreed that government under the Constitution would begin on March 4, 1789
	First Federal Elections

Warming Up

1. Share your research on the "founding fathers" with your classmates.
2. If you were an English military official who still wanted to keep America as colonies, do you think it would be a good chance then to tear up Treaty of Paris and to launch another attack? If there was a good chance, describe the conditions in America.

Historical Highlights

The Ideology of Building a New Country

Now that the North American people had successfully achieved their dreams of rights and lands, figuring out a system of government to run the huge country became a top priority.

Republicanism

The common belief was that America would become a republic—a country which gives more equality to citizens and encourages egalitarian civic-mindedness. This kind of republicanism is based on ancient Roman republic. At the same time, other Americans were developing a different set of ideas that put more attention on ambition and economic freedom.

Confederation

In order to meet the demands of both sides, the government created relatively equal and loose policies. This government system is called the confederate system. Under Confederation, there was just a nominal government which had way of enforcing laws upon the 13 states.

The Articles of Confederation

The Articles more or less put down on paper what had come to exist organically over the previous year, although the main concern at the time was carrying out the war against Great Britain. The document was edited and sent to the states for ratification in 1777.

Structure of Government under the Articles

The Articles called for a one-house, or unicameral, legislature. This Congress would have delegations from each state. Each state delegate would get one vote. Routine decisions required just a simple majority or seven votes. Important decisions required nine votes. Changes and amendments to the document itself required a whole agreement and ratification in Congress. However, the lack of powerful leading government made it hard to agree on political matters. Furthermore, America came with problems of finance, diplomacy, military decisions, and more. The new nation was fragile, and the Articles provided no governmental power to collect taxes, form a military, enforce treaties, etc.

State Constitutions

In May 1776, Continental Congress urged the states to draft constitutions. All the state constitutions affirmed their publican idea and drafted their own laws. These constitutions indicated that governing units should be relatively small. Some constitution created direct democracy or strengthened the lower legislative house. Some established annual elections in the lower house.

Debate Over the Ratification

The development of the Constitution caused people divided into two general political categories.

The Federalists

The supporters of the Constitution labeled themselves Federalists and wrote a series of articles that outlined the failures of the Articles of Confederation and the benefits of a powerful government, with checks and balances.

Anti-Federalists

Anti-federalists were worried that the new government would be controlled by the upper class. They saw the document as a legal way to create a powerful, aristocratic government. They were distrustful of distant authority, as they had been before the Revolution, and were concerned that individual rights would not be adequately protected.

Ratification

Many Anti-federalists refused to support the ratification of the Constitution and insisted on the addition of a list of individual rights that should be clarified. This agreement led to the development of the first ten amendments to the Constitution, known as the Bill of Rights.

Inflation, Debt, and the Rejection of the Impost

The states printed millions of dollars, driving up inflation. In addition, the government borrowed millions of dollars during the war. After the war, the government had trouble paying off these debts. To solve it, the government proposed a 5% tax on all goods imported to raise revenues. But Rhode Island and New York did not want to give up the power, so they rejected the proposed impost.

Organizing the Northwest Territory

Bypassing the Northwest Ordinance and establishing procedures and guidelines, the Confederation Congress made huge progress in incorporating the country's western lands use.

The Northwest Territory

The Northwest land is about the status of the vast swath of land between the Appalachian Mountains and the Mississippi River. Maryland insisted that they should not ratify the Articles until the western lands became part of a national domain.

Land Ordinances and the Northwest Ordinance

The Land Ordinance of 1785, reduced the number of states to between three and five, and called for the area for education. In 1787, the Northwest Ordinance set up a process by which areas could become territories, and then states. Also, the Northwest Ordinance banned slavery in the territory north of the Ohio River.

Foreign Problems

Apart from the domestic issues, the newly-born country is facing a much more severe situation with strong countries set aside. Concerns about the stature of the United States were raised on the world stage. America was in danger of having such a weak central government.

Toward a New Framework for Governance

With these concerns in mind, a group of reformers got approval from Congress to meet and discuss possible changes of the Articles of Confederation. However, it was put down due to the eruption of Shays' Rebellion.

The British and American Indians

The British maintained a thriving fur trade with American Indian groups in the area above the Ohio River. Further, the British provided the natives with weapons. The British also insisted that they would not abandon their western presence until the United States repaid its war debts.

Spain Challenged American Growth in the West

Spain grew increasingly alarmed by the number of American settlers pouring west. It suspected that the growing American population would soon begin to cross into the Louisiana Territory. To discourage American settlement, Spain closed the sea route from Mississippi River to America. Government pressured the Spanish minister to reopen the river but was rejected.

Shays' Rebellion (1786—1787)

Shays' Rebellion (1786—1787) was an outcome of tensions between coastal elites and struggling farmers in the interior. Struggling farmers, unable to pay these taxes, were losing their farms to banks. The farmers petitioned the legislature to pass laws for protection, but it was rejected. Hundreds of Massachusetts farmers protested and finally took up weapons. After several weeks, the governor and legislature took action to suppress the rebellion. Shays' Rebellion showed the public how important a central government was.

The Great Compromise

A major topic for debate was how the various states should be represented in the new government. After much debate, the delegates agreed on the Great Compromise, which created the basic structure of Congress as it now exists. The plan called for a House of Representatives, in which representation would be determined by the population of each state, and a Senate, in which each state would get two members.

Three-Fifths Compromise

Another issue then arose: Whether and how slaves would be counted in determining a state's population? After much debate, a compromise was agreed upon in which southern states could count three-fifths of their slave population in the counting.

Tacit Approval of Slavery

The Constitution provided for the return of fugitive slaves, a process which was strengthened by the Fugitive Slave Act of 1850. Though slavery was not mentioned by name, the inclusion of regulations around slavery made clear its existence.

The Three Branches of Government, Separation of Powers, Checks and Balances

The framers of the Constitution created three separate branches of government. The legislative branch creates laws, the executive branch carries out laws, and the judicial branch interprets laws. The Constitution spells out the powers of each branch. The powers of Congress are enumerated in Article I. These include the power to levy taxes, to regulate trade, to print money, to establish post offices, to declare war, to approve treaties, etc. The powers of the president are included in Article II. These include the power to suggest legislation, to command the armed forces, and to nominate Supreme Court judges. The powers of the judiciary, headed by the Supreme Court, are outlined in Article III. The goal was to keep the three branches in balance so that no single entity gained too much power.

Activating

1. Speech

Suppose you were one of the "founding fathers". You would have a discussion about Confederation in the meeting. As a leader, you need to illustrate your stance and reasons when the nation faced danger. (Since you have become one of the "founding fathers", you need to know the political perspective, personality and position of the person you choose.)

2. Debate

Is federalism legal and suitable to be American political system?

3. Discussion

Please share your opinions on the Compromise.

Exercising

✍ Analyze the extent to which Enlightenment influenced American politics from 1763—1787. (800—1000 words)

The Critical Period **Unit Five**

_____

_____
_____
_____
_____
_____
_____
_____
_____

✎ Analyze the reasons why there would be the change from Confederation to Federalism. (800—1200 words)

_____

_____
_____
_____
_____
_____
_____
_____
_____
_____

Homework

✎ Make a table to illuminate the differences of American politics under Articles of Confederation and Constitution. You can search online. For example:

Legislature	
Confederation	**Constitution**
Unicameral, called Congress	Bicameral, called Congress, divided into the House of Representatives and the Senate

051

- Prepare a speech: How Great Compromise influences the political system.
- Team up and do some research on each state's government during Confederation. Then each team should choose a representative to introduce these states' government system.

Unit Six

Political Parties after American Revolution

1786	Shays' Rebellion
	Annapolis meeting to revise Articles of Confederation
1787	Northwest Ordinance
	Constitutional Convention in Philadelphia
1788	Publication of *The Federalist*
	Ratification of the Constitution
	First federal elections
1789	Inauguration of George Washington
	Judiciary Act
	Beginning of French Revolution
	Publication of *The Interesting Narrative of the Life of Olaudah Equiano, Or Gustavus Vassa, the African*
1791—1794	Whiskey Rebellion
1791	Ratification of the Bill of Rights
	Alexander Hamilton issued Report on Manufacturers
	The Bank of the United States was approved

1793	War between Great Britain and France
	Washington's Proclamation of Neutrality
1795	Jay's Treaty
	Pinckney's Treaty
1796	Washington's Farewell Address
1797	XYZ Affair
1798	Quasi-War with France
	Alien and Sedition Acts
	Kentucky and Virginia Resolutions
1800	Election of Thomas Jefferson
1803	Louisiana Purchase
	Marbury v. Madison
1804	Reelection of Thomas Jefferson
1807	Chesapeake-Leopard affair
	Embargo Act
1808	Election of James Madison
1810	Fletcher v. Peck
1811	Battle of Tippecanoe
1812	Beginning of the War of 1812
	Reelection of Madison
1814	Hartford Convention

Political Parties after American Revolution — Unit Six

	Treaty of Ghent
1815	Battle of New Orleans
1816	Election of James Monroe
	Chartering of the Second Bank of the United States
1817	Construction of Erie Canal begins
1819	Panic of 1819
	Dartmouth College v. Woodward
	McCulloch v. Maryland
1820	Missouri Compromise
	Election of James Monroe
1821	Cohen's v. Virginia
1822	Stephen F. Austin established first American settlement in Texas
1824	Gibbons v. Ogden
	Election of John Quincy Adams
1825	Opening of the Erie Canal
1827	Public school movement began in Boston
1828	Passage of the "Tariff of Abominations"
	Election of Andrew Jackson
1829	Publication of David Walker's *Appeal to the Coloured Citizens of the World*
1830	Opening of the Baltimore and Ohio Railroad
	Passage of the Indian Removal Act

1830—1850	Founding of Mormonism "Trail of Tears"
1831	William Lloyd Garrison began publication of *The Liberator*
	Cherokee Nation v. Georgia
1832	Beginning of Nullification Crisis
	Andrew Jackson vetoed renewal of Second Bank of the United States
	Worcester v. Georgia
1833	Founding of the American Anti-Slavery Society
1834	Whig Party organized the first strike by the "Lowell girls"
1835	Publication of Alexis de Tocqueville's *Democracy in America*
1836	Congress passed the "gag rule"
	Andrew Jackson issued Specie Circular
	The Battle of the Alamo and Texas Declaration of Independence
1837	Elijah Parish Lovejoy was murdered by pro-slavery mob

The first dozen years after the ratification of the Constitution were of great significance in the shaping of the United States politically. The government and country were coming to terms with the implementation of the Constitution. The Bill of Rights established important civil liberties. It was in this period that many of the American political system's traditions and precedents—collectively known as the "unwritten constitution"—were established. We see the development of political parties and of the bipartisan system during these years. Furthermore, we see continuing struggles over the new nation's identity.

Political Parties after American Revolution Unit Six

Warming Up

1. These men are considered the most important figures of the United States. Can you recognize them? Try giving a brief introduction on them.

2. The pictures below show some artistic works about the remarkable figures in American history. These works are not only about leadership, but also about political conflicts and humanity. Exchange your personal opinions with classmates.

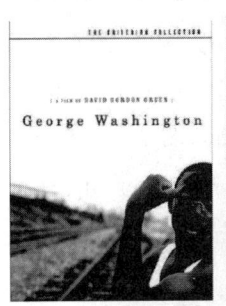

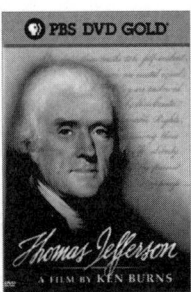

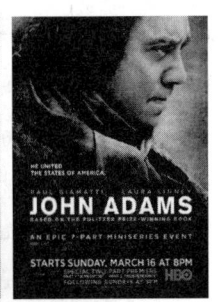

057

George Washington is a 1984 television miniseries directed by Buzz Kulik.

Thomas Jefferson is a 1997 two-part American documentary film which covers the life and times of Thomas Jefferson, the 3rd President of the United States.

Hamilton is a musical about the life of American Founding Father Alexander Hamilton.

John Adams is a 2008 American television miniseries chronicling most of U.S. President John Adams's political life and his role in the founding of the United States.

Historical Highlights

The Federalist Era

The Federalist Era lasted roughly from 1789 to 1801, when the Federalist Party dominated and shaped American politics. This era saw the adoption of the United States Constitution and the growth of a strong centralized government. The period was also characterized by foreign tensions and conflict with France and England, as well as internal opposition from the rival Democratic-Republicans.

The dynamic force behind the Federalist Party during Washington's presidency was Alexander Hamilton. Hamilton devised a complex, multifaceted program to achieve his vision of a strong centralized government and diverse economy. One of his policies was the assumption of each state's debts from the Revolutionary War. "A national debt," Hamilton concluded, "will be to us a national blessing...powerful cement to our union." He also proposed a novel system of taxes and tariffs to pay for the debt and a Bank of the United States to handle the finances and centralize the fiscal resources of the federal government. Hamilton also designed policies that encouraged manufacturing and commerce, leading to the growth of a wealthy, urban merchant class.

The Unwritten Constitution

The term "unwritten constitution" refers to the processes of American government that are considered an essential part of the system but are not actually in the Constitution. These are customs and precedents that have been in place for so long that many citizens think these are, in fact, laws, but are not. As the first president of the United States, George Washington made great contributions to the customs of American politics.

The Cabinet

George Washington's first task as President of the United States was to appoint Secretaries (heads) of each of the executive departments. He appointed Alexander Hamilton Secretary of the Treasury, John Jay Secretary of State until Thomas Jefferson returned from Europe and Henry Knox was made Secretary of War. John Adams was the Vice President. Washington took things a step further when he called regular meetings to get the advice of these men. He therefore created what became known as the Cabinet. The formation of a cabinet to advise the president is a precedent set by George Washington. The Constitution neither required nor suggested Washington do this. Since then every president has followed Washington's precedent. Today the cabinet is much larger and comprises of the heads of the various federal agencies and departments as well as key advisers.

Term Limits for President

To understand how important the unwritten constitution has become one might cite the example of the two-term limit. The first President George Washington refused to run for a third term. He felt that to rule for longer than two terms might give one man too much power and influence. In doing so he set a precedent that was followed until Theodore Roosevelt. Roosevelt also followed the precedent set and when he was finished with his second term did not run again. A young man Roosevelt continued to be active in his political party. When Taft was President, Roosevelt became enraged at the way the new President did things. In response he ran for president under a new third party named the "Bull Moose Party." In 1951, the Constitution was amended to include a two-term limit for the Presidency.

Bill of Rights—Amendments to the Constitution

The Bill of Rights is the collective name for the first ten amendments to the United States Constitution. Proposed following the oftentimes bitter 1787—1788 battle over ratification of the U.S. Constitution, and crafted to address the objections raised by anti-Federalists, the Bill of Rights amendments add to the Constitution specific guarantees of personal freedoms and rights, clear limitations on the government's power in judicial and other proceedings, and explicit declarations that all powers not specifically delegated to Congress by the Constitution are reserved for the states or the people.

Hamilton's Program—The American System

In the aftermath of ratification, George Washington became the first President of the United States in 1789 and appointed Hamilton as Secretary of the Treasury. In his new role,

Hamilton continued to expand on his interpretations of the Constitution to defend a series of proposed economic policies.

The United States began to become mired in debt. In 1789, when Hamilton took up his post, the federal debt was over $53 million. The states had a combined debt of around $25 million, and the United States had been unable to pay its debts in the 1780s and was therefore considered a credit risk by European countries. Credited today with creating the foundation for the U.S. financial system, Hamilton wrote three reports offering solutions to the economic crisis brought on by these problems. The first addressed public credit, the second addressed banking, and the third addressed raising revenue.

In his vision of strong central government, Hamilton demonstrated little sympathy for state autonomy or a fear of excessive central authority. Instead, he believed that the United States should emulate Britain's strong central political structure and encourage the growth of commerce, trade alliances, and manufacturing. In response to the debate over whether or not Congress had the authority to establish a national bank, for example, Hamilton wrote the *Defense of the Constitutionality of the Bank*, which forcefully argued that Congress could choose any means not explicitly prohibited by the Constitution to achieve a constitutional end—even if the means by which this was accomplished were deemed unconstitutional.

Hamilton justified the Bank and the broad scope of congressional power necessary to establish it by citing Congress' constitutional powers to issue currency, regulate interstate commerce, and enact any other legislation "necessary and proper" to put into practice the provisions of the Constitution. This broad view of congressional power was enshrined into legal precedent in the Supreme Court case McCulloch v. Maryland, which granted the federal government broad freedom to select the best means to execute its constitutionally enumerated powers. This ruling has since been termed the "doctrine of implied powers," in regards to the specified powers of the federal government in the Constitution.

Innovation in manufacturing, as demonstrated in the development of the "American System," was extolled by Hamilton and the Federalist Party in the 1790s as the supreme virtues of American republicanism. The "American System" featured semi-skilled labor using machine tools and jigs to make standardized, identical, interchangeable parts, which could be assembled with a minimum of time and skill. Since the parts were interchangeable, it became possible to separate manufacturing from assembly, which could then be carried out by semi-skilled labor on an assembly line—an example of the division of labor. The system allowed industrialists to greatly reduce costs.

In his *Report on Manufacturers*, Hamilton argued that an expansion of manufacturing (particularly of textiles) was necessary to produce nationally-made goods—and thereby reduce American dependence on European products. Arguing that continued dependence on Europe for manufactured goods jeopardized U.S. independence, Hamilton encouraged Congress to implement protective tariffs, invest in new mechanization processes and technical innovations, import foreign technicians and laborers to foster mechanization, and encourage loans for business entrepreneurs.

Furthermore, Hamilton and the Federalists believed that the characteristics of the successful industrialists—self-reliance, autonomy, innovation, and entrepreneurship—were the bedrock of values on which they sought to model the national political system. According to Hamilton, the commercial classes created a class of talented, industrious, and virtuous men who could be trusted to wield federal political power. Hence, for the Federalists, manufacturing was of primary importance to federal policy because it served as a breeding ground for new generations of talented, virtuous republican leaders.

As opposed to his Democratic-Republican contemporaries who espoused agriculture and farming as the backbone of the American economy, Hamilton believed that overall commercial development would foster the republican virtues of self-reliance and autonomy, as well as American independence in the world economic system. Hamilton's distinctive lack of an agricultural policy, in favor of this commercial plan, alienated him from some of his political contemporaries; however, his vision for American manufacturing later influenced the development of the United States' textile industry after the invention of the cotton gin increased American cotton cultivation in the 1800s.

In order to build support for his program, Hamilton led a coalition of supporters anchored by prominent Northeastern businessmen and financiers. This network grew into the Federalist Party to express their support of a strong central government and legitimize their claims that they were the true supporters of the Constitution. Broadly interpreting the powers of the federal government under the "necessary and proper" clause of the Constitution, Hamilton's policies were approved by the Federalist-dominated Congress as well as by President Washington.

The Whiskey Rebellion

As part of his economic policies designed to address the national debt, Hamilton urged Congress to impose a tax on domestically distilled liquors, a "luxury tax" that he believed would not cause much consternation in the American public. Farmers on the western frontier operated private distilleries to generate extra income, and for many poor farmers, whiskey was a medium of exchange, rather than cash. For these farmers, the whiskey tax constituted an unfair income tax that privileged wealthy farmers and eastern distilleries who could afford to pay a flat tax per barrel.

In 1794, outbursts of violence against tax assessors in western Pennsylvania resulted in a large mob of poor farmers who demanded independence from the United States, motivated by other economic grievances as well as the whiskey tax. President Washington sent a militia of over 12,000 men to subdue the rebellion, which occurred without bloodshed. Washington later pardoned the two rebels who were convicted of treason, and the tax was repealed in 1802.

The Washington administration's suppression of the Whiskey Rebellion was met with widespread popular approval and demonstrated the new national government had the willingness and ability to suppress violent resistance to its laws. Historians such as Steven Boyd have argued that the suppression of the Whiskey Rebellion prompted anti-Federalist Westerners to finally accept the Constitution and to seek change by voting rather than resisting the government. Federalists, for their part, came to accept that the people could play a greater role in governance.

French Revolution and Neutrality

In 1789, the French Revolution broke out, sending shock waves through Europe and the United States. From 1789 to 1792, as the French overthrew their monarchy and declared a republic, many Americans supported the revolution. Democratic-Republicans seized on the French revolutionaries' struggle against monarchy as the welcome harbinger of a larger republican movement around the world. To the Federalists, however, the French Revolution represented pure anarchy, especially after the execution of the French king in 1793. Along with other foreign and domestic uprisings, the French Revolution helped harden the political divide in the United States in the early 1790s.

The controversy in the United States intensified when France declared war on Great Britain and Holland in February 1793. France requested that the United States make a large repayment of the money it had borrowed from France to fund the Revolutionary War. However, Great Britain would judge any aid given to France as a hostile act.

Apprehensive of foreign entanglements and war, President Washington's official policy was one of neutrality. He knew that England or France, as well as Spain, would be quick to seize American resources and territory if given the excuse of war. His hope was that America could stay out of European conflicts until it was strong enough to withstand any serious foreign threat to its existence. Therefore, despite the mutual defense treaty the United States established with France in 1778, Washington and the Federalists declared that the Revolution rendered previous agreements with France non-binding, and issued a formal Proclamation of Neutrality in 1793. Democratic-Republican groups, however, denounced neutrality and declared their support of the French republicans. The Federalists used the violence of the French revolutionaries as a reason to attack Democratic-Republicanism in the United States, arguing that Jefferson and Madison would lead the country down a similarly disastrous path.

Jay's Treaty

During the 1790s, the British Royal Navy began encroaching on United States neutrality by pressing sailors into service from American commercial ships. Although the majority of sailors impressed into the British navy were English citizens working for higher wages and better standards of living for American merchants, this violation of the American flag infuriated Americans; this was compounded by the fact that England had not yet withdrawn its soldiers from posts in the Northwest Territory, as required by the Treaty of Paris of 1783.

In response, President Washington sent John Jay to negotiate a treaty with England. Jay's Treaty, signed in 1794, guaranteed the removal of British forces from forts in the Northwest Territories, committed disputes over wartime debts to arbitration, gave the U.S. limited trading rights with British colonies, and restricted U.S. cotton exports. Although Jay's Treaty helped prevent war with England, it provoked an outcry among American citizens who saw it as a concession to England. The Senate narrowly ratified Jay's Treaty, but the debate it sparked solidified the Federalist and Democratic-Republican factions into full-scale political parties.

The Northwest Indian War

The Northwest Indian War, or Little Turtle's War, resulted from the exacerbation of conflict between the United States and the Western Confederacy over occupation of the Northwest Territory. During the 1780s and 1790s, British agents in the region continued to sell weapons and ammunition to the American Indians, encouraging attacks on European American invaders. Invaders retaliated with equally violent attacks on American Indians. In response to this escalation, President George Washington and Secretary of War Henry Knox ordered General Josiah Harmar to launch a major western offensive into the Shawnee and Miami country, beginning in October of 1790. After initial losses under Colonel Hardin and Major General St. Clair, Washington ordered General Anthony Wayne to form a well-trained force and subdue the American Indian forces. After extensive training, Wayne's troops advanced into the territory and built Fort Recovery at the site of St. Clair's defeat. Wayne's well-trained legion continued to advance deeper into the territory of the Wabash Confederacy, and the last of the American Indian forces were defeated at the Battle of Fallen Timbers in August 1794.

The Treaty of Greenville

Following the battle, the Western Confederacy and the United States signed the Treaty of Greenville on August 3, 1795 to end the Northwest Indian War. In exchange for goods to the value of $20,000, the American Indian tribes were forced to cede most of the areas of Ohio and Indiana and to formally recognize the United States as the ruling power in the Old Northwest. The treaty also established what became known as the "Greenville Treaty Line," which was for several years a boundary between American Indian territory and lands open to European-American invaders; however the latter frequently disregarded the treaty line as they continued to encroach on native lands west of the boundary.

The Alien and Sedition Acts of 1798

The decisive event that signalled the collapse of the Federalist Party was the passage of the Alien and Sedition Acts during the presidency of Federalist John Adams. These acts consisted of a series of legislative "protective" acts to prevent "aliens" with subversive intentions from spreading the insidious elements of the French Revolution to the United States, as well as to prevent "malicious" publications or seditious speeches by Federalist opponents. The Alien and Sedition Acts were denounced by Democratic-Republicans as a direct assault on freedom of speech and the right to organized legislative opposition to the current administration.

Age of Jeffersonian Republican

Known informally as the Jeffersonian Republicans, this group of politicians organized in opposition to the policies of Federalists such as Alexander Hamilton, who favored a strong central government.

Led by Thomas Jefferson, whom they helped elect as president for two terms (1801—1809), the Republicans believed in individual freedoms and the rights of states. They feared that the concentration of federal power under George Washington and John Adams represented a dangerous threat to liberty. In foreign policy, the Republicans favored France, which had supported the Colonies during the Revolution, over Great Britain.

These ideas represented a departure from the policies of the Federalists under the administrations of Washington and Adams. The Federalists had established monetary policies that gave more power to the federal government and had rejected ties with France in favor of closer links to Britain.

The Rise of Political Parties

Debates over Hamilton's economic program, French Revolution and the Whiskey Rebellion finally led United States to develop two distinct political parties—Federalists and Democratic Republican. Federalists, led by Hamilton and John Adams, favored a strong centralized government and wanted to base economy on industry and trade. Democratic Republican, led by Jefferson and Madison, thought states should have more power and wanted to base the economy on farming.

Election of 1800

Jefferson and another candidate, Aaron Burr, drew a tie in the voting process. Then, as the Constitution requires, the House of Representative had to decide between the two. Hamilton trusted Jefferson's political leadership and therefore the Federalists allowed Jefferson to become the President. In 1804, Burr killed Hamilton in a duel.

Jefferson Simplicity

Jefferson encouraged Congress to abandon the Alien and Sedition Acts and lower the taxes on stamps, land and alcohol. Besides, Jefferson cut the national debt from $80 million to $57 million by reducing the size of the federal government. He also focused on the independent farmers and freedom of speech.

Louisiana Purchase

In the hope to gain more land for growing population, Jefferson decided to buy Louisiana Territory from France at the price of $15 million in 1803. However, this action was against Jefferson's idea of strict interpretation of the Constitution. Overall, this purchase is beneficial for America in both land size and trade (New Orleans was the important port for trade). Today, Louisiana Purchase turns out to be one of the most remarkable contributions of Jefferson.

Madison's Presidency

In the presidential election of 1808, James Madison defeated Federalist candidate to become the nation's fourth president. Madison issued the Non-Intercourse Act of 1809 which allowed to open trade to all countries except Britain and France. Later, he also issued Macon's

Bill Number 2 and stopped trade with Britain because France agreed to accept American neutral status at sea. However, as the failure of these foreign policies, Madison led nation into the War of 1812 against Britain.

War of 1812

Trade conflicts and pressure from the War Hawks, congressmen who pushed war against Britain, let Madison declare war against Britain in 1812. Although most regions agreed to the war, Federalists and New England merchants didn't agree due to trade profits. During the war, which lasted two and a half years, there are some important events. These events are British invasion of New York, Battle of Lake Champlain, the burning of the White House and Battle of New Orleans in 1814.

Finally, the war of 1812 ended with the Treaty of Ghent (1814). The relationship between Britain and America was same as the one before the war. Also, the war helped to build a sense of nationalism and increased America's ability to focus on internal improvements in infrastructure and industry.

Era of Good Feelings

The Era of Good Feelings marked a period in the political history of the United States that reflected a sense of national purpose and a desire for unity among Americans in the aftermath of the War of 1812. The era saw a brief lull in the bitter partisan disputes that had plagued the Democratic-Republican and Federalist parties. President James Monroe endeavored to consolidate the Democratic-Republican and Federalist parties, with the ultimate goal of eliminating parties altogether from national politics.

Henry Clay

Leader of the Whig party and five times an unsuccessful presidential candidate, Henry Clay (1777—1852) played a central role on the stage of national politics for over forty years. He was secretary of state under John Quincy Adams, Speaker of the House of Representatives longer than anyone else in the nineteenth century, and the most influential member of the Senate during its golden age. In a parliamentary system, he would have undoubtedly become prime minister.

Corrupt Bargain

The 1824 presidential election marked the final collapse of the Republican-Federalist political framework. For the first time no candidate ran as a Federalist, while five significant candidates competed as Democratic-Republicans. Clearly, no party system functioned in

1824.

The outcome of the very close election surprised political leaders. The winner in the all-important Electoral College was Andrew Jackson, the hero of the War of 1812, with ninety-nine votes. He was followed by John Quincy Adams, the son of the second president and Monroe' secretary of state, who secured eighty-four votes. Although Jackson seemed to have won a narrow victory, receiving 43 percent of the popular vote versus just 30 percent for Adams, he would not be seated as the country's sixth president. Because nobody had received a majority of votes in the electoral college, the House of Representatives had to choose between the top two candidates.

Henry Clay, the speaker of the House of Representatives, now held a decisive position. As a presidential candidate himself in 1824 (he finished fourth in the electoral college), Clay had led some of the strongest attacks against Jackson. Rather than see the nation's top office go to a man he detested, the Kentuckian Clay forged an Ohio Valley-New England coalition that secured the White House for John Quincy Adams. In return Adams named Clay as his secretary of state, a position that had been the stepping-stone to the presidency for the previous four executives.

This arrangement, however, hardly proved beneficial for either Adams or Clay. Denounced immediately as a "corrupt bargain" by supporters of Jackson, the antagonistic presidential race of 1828 began practically before Adams even took office.

After losing the presidency to Andrew Jackson in 1828, John Quincy Adams was elected to the House of Representatives where he served until his death in 1848.

Jacksonian Democratic

Jacksonian Democracy was the prevailing political philosophy in the United States in the 1820s to 1840s, embodied in the the policies of President Andrew Jackson and his followers in the new Democratic Party. Historians coined the term to recognize Jackson's primary role, and to include both democracy (the rule of the people) and Democrats (a common name for members of the Democratic Party).

Spoils System

A spoils system, also called a patronage system, was a practice in which the political party winning an election rewarded its campaign workers and other active supporters by appointment to government posts and by other favors. During Jackson's presidency, he hired his supporters to serve as government officials, which is criticized much nowadays.

Indian Removal Act

The Indian Removal Act was signed into law by President Andrew Jackson on May 28, 1830, authorizing the president to grant unsettled lands west of the Mississippi River in exchange for Indian lands within existing state borders. A few tribes went peacefully, but many resisted the relocation policy. The Supreme Court ruled that Indian tribes were indeed sovereign and immune from Georgia laws. President Jackson nonetheless refused to heed the Court's decision. During the following years, tens if not hundreds of thousands of Native Americans were forced or coerced to leave their lands. Thousands died from disease, malnourishment, and mistreatment during forced marches across thousands of miles.

Nullification Crisis

The Nullification Crisis emerged due to issues of sectional strife with disagreements over tariffs. Critics alleged that high tariffs on imports of common manufactured goods made in Europe made those goods more expensive than ones from the northern U.S., raising the prices paid by planters in the South. Southern politicians argued that tariffs benefited northern industrialists at the expense of southern farmers.

The issue came to a head when Vice President Calhoun supported the claim of his home state, South Carolina, that it had the right to nullify the tariff legislation of 1828, and more generally the right of a state to nullify any Federal laws that went against its interests. In response to South Carolina's nullification claim, Jackson vowed to send troops to South Carolina to enforce the laws.

Destruction of the Second National Bank

Jackson, believing that Bank was fundamentally a corrupt monopoly whose stock was mostly held by foreigners vetoed the bill. Jackson used the issue to promote his democratic values, believing the Bank was being run exclusively for the wealthy. Jackson stated the Bank made "the rich richer and the potent more powerful". In 1833, Jackson removed federal deposits from the bank, whose money-lending functions were taken over by the legions of local and state banks that materialized across America, thus drastically increasing credit and speculation. Three years later, Jackson issued the Specie Circular, an executive order that required buyers of government lands to pay in "specie" (gold or silver coins). The result was a great demand for specie, which many banks did not have enough of to exchange for their notes, causing the Panic of 1837, which threw the national economy into a deep depression.

Political Parties after American Revolution Unit Six

Activating

1. Presentation

Each student will have a five-minute presentation to talk about which man we mentioned before you would choose to be the president and why.

2. Debate

Please prepare a debate among three parties. One point that shall be involved in the debate are core policies about the government power and states power.

Exercising

✍ Please analyze the reason behind the change of power among parties. (500—800 words)

✍ What's your opinion about the power balance between states and central government? (Should state has more power or central government, how to better assign power, etc.)

069

✍ Make a table to compare and contrast three political parties (Federalists, Democratic Republican and Jacksonian Democratic).

Homework

✍ Choose your favorite figure among all men we have mentioned in class and write him a song. You can take a look at relevant documents for inspiration.

✍ Choose one of the founding fathers to be your friend. Introduce the reason why you would choose him. This task is to show your full understanding towards their personalities, features and backgrounds.

✍ You are going to make propaganda for one of the parties. Remember to include the necessary details such as the leader of the party and the slogan in the propaganda. Some research on the art and literature of the time will be very helpful for you to create an antique propaganda.

✍ As one of the officials of the three parties, you need to prepare a speech to the public to spread your political beliefs.

✍ Imagine that Napoleon along with his government officials met Washington who also brought his crew on the bank of Seine River. They talked about their own country's political system, citizens, industry, art, literature and some other topics you may think of. Present a drama as a whole to show the historic meeting.

Unit Seven

Market Revolution and Whig Party

1840	Election of William Henry Harrison of the Whig Party
	Formation of the Liberty Party
1841	John Tyler assumed presidency upon Harrison's death
	Brook Farm was founded
	Dorothea Dix organized movement for asylum reform
1844	Samuel Morse invented the telegraph and sent his first telegraph message

Warming Up

1. If you were a businessman/businesswoman now, and you were suffering from an economic crisis, what actions would you expect the government to do? You can refer to the 2008 economic crisis and give us your opinions.

2. America has gone through an economic transformation from Hamilton to Henry Clay. Deduct what will economic developing pattern be like in the next period?

Historical Highlights

Changes in Infrastructure

Improvements in Transportation

Upgrades in transportation made production for distant markets possible. By 1850, the eastern half of the United States was crisscrossed by a series of roads, canals, and railroads. People moved goods from city to city, back and forth from coastline to inland. This caused a huge economic boom.

Canals and Roads

The first set of improvements, including the expansion and improvement of roads and canals and the development of the steamboat, helped much to expand trade between the midwest and eastern cities. Construction took place from 1811 to 1853. But soon these finished inventions were overshadowed by the railroad.

Railroads

The Baltimore and Ohio Railroad is recognized as the first licensed common carrier railroad in the United States. The government encouraged the construction of the railroad by granting railroad companies an agreeable proportion of land. The government's fund also enriched the railroad companies. All these transportation improvements paved the way for the nation's economic expansion.

Advances in Communications

The major advance in communications was the electronic communication. The first telegraph line was from Washington DC to Baltimore. The messages were transmitted in Morse code. By 1850, telegraph lines became lifeline of the country. The telegraph greatly fed the development of a national market of products and services.

Systematic Changes

Slater Mill and the Development of the Factory System

America began to move towards the industrial mass production of goods. The first field to industrialize was the textile industry. Factory system became mature and contributed to the rising of working class and laid the foundation for women rights.

The Incorporation of America

After 1810, chartering of business was allowed by states. Incorporation encouraged investment into the corporation and protected the individual investors from personal legal liability for mistakes or crimes of the corporation.

The Supreme Court and the Market Economy

Supreme Court decisions in the first half of the nineteenth century tended to support and define the rules of the growing market economy. The Supreme Court granted corporations unprecedented rights in economic activities. Benefiting from the market in the following decades, the number of corporations and investors grew dramatically.

The Expansion of Banking

The panic of 1819 demonstrated the instability of market economy. However, the remarkable growth afterwards formed a new economy. Second Bank of the United States extended credit and issued bank notes. The ability of banks to put currency into the economy fueled economic growth.

The Promise and the Limits of the "American System"

The market economy finally created stronger links between the North and Midwest, while the South became increasingly isolated from the rest of the country.

Henry Clay's "American System"

Following the War of 1812, Henry Clay proposed what he later called the "American System" to provoke economic growth. The policies included "internal improvements" in transportation, putting high tariffs on imported goods and chartering a Second Bank of the United States to stabilize the economy and to make credit more readily available.

Whig Party

Whig Party was a political party active in the middle of the 19th century in the United States. Whig Party rose mainly because of the mutual opposition among members against President Jackson. More Specifically, the Whigs supported the dominance of Congress over the presidential power and favored modernization, banking and economic protectionism. It benefited entrepreneurs and planters, but had fewer effects on farmers or workers. The Whig Party nominated several presidential candidates including Henry Clay.

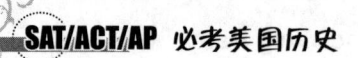

The Growth of Cotton Production

In the first half of the nineteenth century, cotton became the most profitable crop in the South. The profitability of southern cotton contributed to a dramatic growth in slavery in the first half of the nineteenth century and an expansion of the internal slave trade. The invention of the cotton gin allowed for the rapid processing of cotton. With insatiable demand for cotton, production increased at a rapid pace.

King Cotton, North and South

The increase in cotton production benefited both South and North. In the north, cotton was used as main resources for cloth in New England. By 1860, 58 percent of American exports ran business of cotton. Cotton was then called "King Cotton." As cotton production increased, the number of slaves in the South also increased.

Cotton and Slavery

Slavery become dominant in the South just as it was becoming unpopular in the world. The United States outlawed the international slave trade which had been protected by the Constitution until 1808. All of the northern states had voted to abolish slavery entirely or gradually.

Activating

1. Presentation

If you were one of the members who was to solve the 2008 crisis, what rescue plan will you take? Please make a brief plan and explain reasons within 3 minutes.

2. Debate

Does the economic crisis have a positive or a negative influence?

3. Drama

Please prepare a drama about the market revolution period. The content of the drama should be the relationships and the thoughts among men and women in a factory system.

Market Revolution and Whig Party — Unit Seven

Exercising

✍ If you were one of the responsible personnel, how would you balance the public religion belief and the current economy?

_____
_____
_____
_____
_____
_____
_____
_____
_____
_____

✍ Please assess the impacts of market revolution in different perspectives and predict the developing pattern of it.

_____
_____
_____
_____
_____
_____
_____
_____
_____
_____
_____

Homework

✍ Would the economic crisis still happen if Hamilton did not launch his plan or there was no Hamilton?

✍ Assuming that you were a merchant, how would you design your trading route if you want to have trade in different regions? Explain it.

✍ Please do a research on the wake of religion during this period and share it with everyone in next class.

Unit Eight

Antebellum Culture

1844	Samuel Morse invented the telegraph and sent his first message
	James Polk was elected president
1845	Texas annexation
1846	Creation of the Independent Treasury
	Resolution of dispute with Great Britain over Oregon Territory
	Beginning of Mexican War
1848	Seneca Falls Convention
	Treaty of Guadalupe Hidalgo ended Mexican War
	Gold found in California
1850	Compromise of 1850
1851—1852	Publication of *Uncle Tom's Cabin*, by Harriet Beecher Stowe
1851	Herman Melville writes *Moby-Dick*
1854	Ostend Manifesto
	Beginning of "Bleeding Kansas"
1856	The beating of Senator Charles Sumner
1857	Dred Scott v. Sanford decision
1859	John Brown's raid on Harper's Ferry arsenal

Warming Up

1. Some great literary masterpieces focus on the conflicts in human developing process, i.e., environment vs. technology, vice vs. virtue. Have you watched the movie or read the book *Angels and Demons*? Can you summarize the main conflict discussed in the movie/book?

2. Have you read any other books/articles about the conflict shown in the movie above? Some scientists devoted their whole life to experiments and discoveries in order to prove/disprove the existence of God. How can you understand the conflict between material and religion?

3. The Market Revolution inherently encouraged economic and social aggressiveness. Do you think the conflict we've discussed above (technology vs. spirit, material vs. religion) would be apparent during and after Market Revolution? Why?

Historical Highlights

Antebellum Culture

The Antebellum Period in American history is generally considered to be the period before the Civil War and after the War of 1812, although some historians expand it to all the years from the adoption of the Constitution in 1789 to the beginning of the Civil War. It was characterized by the move towards abolition and the gradual polarization of the country between abolitionists and supporters of slavery. At the same time, the country's economy began shifting in the north to manufacturing as the Industrial Revolution began, while in the south, a cotton boom made plantations the center of the existing agrarian economy.

The Second Great Awakening

By the beginning of the 19th century, traditional Christian beliefs were held in less favor by numerous educated Americans. A countervailing tendency was underway, however, in the form of a tremendous religious revival that spread westward during the first half of the century. It coincided with the nation's population explosion from 5 to 30 million and the borders' westward movement.

This Second Great Awakening, a reprise of the Great Awakening of the early 18th century, was marked by an emphasis on personal piety over schooling and theology. It arose in several places and in several active forms. In northern New England, social activism took precedence; in western New York, the movement encouraged the growth of new denominations.

The revival's secular effects consisted of two main strains: The virtues and behavior of the expanding middle class—a strong work ethic, frugality and temperance—were endorsed and legitimized; its emphasis on the ability of individuals to amend their lives engendered a wide array of reform movements aimed at redressing injustice and alleviating suffering—a democratizing effect.

Moral Reforms

Moral reform prior to the Civil War came largely out of this new devotion to religion. Efforts to apply Christian teaching to the resolution of social problems presaged the Social Gospel of the late 19th century. Converts were taught that to achieve salvation, they needed not just to repent of personal sin but also work for the moral perfection of society, which meant eradicating sin in all its forms. Thus, evangelical converts were leading figures in a variety of 19th century reform movements.

Reforms took the shape of social movements for temperance, womens' rights, and the abolition of slavery. Social activists began efforts to reform prisons and care for the handicapped and mentally ill. They believed in the perfectibility of people and were highly moralistic in their endeavors. Many participants in the revival meetings believed that reform was a part of God's plan. As a result, local churches saw their role in society as purifying the world through the individuals to whom they could bring salvation, as well as through changes in the law and the creation of institutions. Interest in transforming the world was applied to political action, as temperance activists, antislavery advocates, and proponents of other variations of reform sought to implement their beliefs into national politics. While religion had previously played an important role on the American political scene, the Second Great Awakening highlighted the important role which individual beliefs would play.

Women Rights of the 19th Century

The movement for women rights in the United States can be traced back to the late 18th and early 19th centuries. First-wave feminism refers to the feminist movement of the 19th through early 20th centuries, which focused mainly on women's suffrage, or right to vote.

During the early part of the 19th century, agitation for equal suffrage was attempted by only a few individuals. The first of these was Frances Wright, a Scottish woman who came to the country in 1826 and advocated women's suffrage in an extensive series of lectures. In 1836, a Polish woman named Ernestine Rose came to the country and undertook a similar campaign so effectively that she obtained a personal hearing before the New York Legislature, though her petition bore only five signatures. In 1840, Lucretia Mott and Margaret Fuller became active in Boston, the latter being the author of the book *The Great Lawsuit: Man vs. Men, Woman vs. Women*. Gerrit Smith, who was the Liberty Party's candidate for president in 1848, successfully championed a plank in his party's position calling for women's equal rights.

The Rise of Abolitionism

Throughout the first half of the 19th century, abolitionism—a movement to end slavery—intensified throughout the United States. In the 1850s, slavery was established legally in the fifteen states constituting the American South. It remained especially strong in plantation areas where crops such as cotton, sugar, tobacco, and hemp were essential exports. By 1860, the slave population in the United States had grown to four million. While American abolitionism strengthened in the North, support for slavery held strong among white Southerners, who profited so greatly from the system of enslaved labor that slavery itself became intertwined with the national economy. The banking, shipping, and manufacturing industries of New York City all had strong economic interests in slavery, as did other major cities in the North.

David Walker

David Walker was a vocal African-American activist who published *Walker's Appeal, in Four Articles* in 1829, attacking slavery as a moral evil and calling on Africans to fight back. Walker saw a need for violence in bringing an end to slavery. A quote from his appeal reads,

"They want us for their slaves, and think nothing of murdering us...therefore, if there is an attempt made by us, kill or be killed...and believe this, that it is no more harm for you to kill a man who is trying to kill you, than it is for you to take a drink of water when thirsty."

Walker stated that Africans deserved to be seen as both humans and Americans. His *Appeal* obviously frightened slave owners, but it also frightened opponents of slavery in the North because it embraced violence. Shortly after the *Appeal*'s publication, Walker was found dead. His Appeal paved the way for future Abolitionists and inspired the movement.

William Lloyd Garrison

Garrison was one of the men inspired by David Walker. He started publishing an anti-slavery newspaper called *The Liberator* in 1831. This is what most consider the formal start of the abolitionist movement.

Garrison was a devoutly Christian man, and he saw slavery as a mortal sin that could not be justified by economics or politics. In 1833, he brought together people in New England to form the American Anti-Slavery Society. The group included Quakers, evangelical Christians who opposed slavery, and other abolitionists. They pushed for an immediate end to slavery and equal rights for free blacks. Unlike Walker, they refused to advocate violence to end slavery.

Frederick Douglass

Frederick Douglass was an escaped slave. He used his excellent abilities as a writer and orator to bring attention to the evil of slavery. Douglass' publication was called the *North Star*. He agreed with the abolitionist stand against violence, but his speeches to white audiences were very blunt. On July 5, 1852 in a New York speech he asked, "Why am I called upon to speak here today? What have I, or those I represent, to do with your national independence? Are the great principles of political freedom and of natural justice, embodied in that Declaration of Independence, extended to us?"

The Rise of the Temperance Movement

In the late 18th century, the early temperance movement sparked to life with Benjamin Rush's 1784 tract, *An Inquiry into the Effects of Spirituous Liquors on the Human Body and the Mind*, which judged the excessive use of alcohol as injurious to physical and psychological health. Influenced by this inquiry, about 200 farmers in a Connecticut community formed a temperance association in 1789 to ban the making of whiskey. Similar associations were formed in Virginia in 1800 and New York in 1808.

Over the next decade, other temperance organizations were formed in eight states, some of which were state-wide organizations. Economic change and urbanization in the early 19th century were accompanied by increasing poverty, and various factors contributed to a widespread increase in alcohol use. Advocates for temperance argued that such alcohol use went hand-in-hand with spousal abuse, family neglect, and chronic unemployment. Americans increasingly drank more strong, cheap alcoholic beverages like rum and whiskey, and pressure for cheap and plentiful alcohol led to relaxed ordinances on alcohol sales, which temperance advocates sought to reform.

The movement advocated temperance, or levelness, rather than abstinence. Many leaders of the movement expanded their activities and took positions on observance of the Sabbath and other moral issues. The reform movements met with resistance by brewers and distillers; many business owners were even fearful of women having the right to vote because it was expected that they would tend to vote for temperance.

Nativism

As German and Irish immigrants poured into the United States in the decades preceding the Civil War, native-born laborers also found themselves competing for jobs with new arrivals who were more likely to be exploited to work longer hours for less pay. This job competition resulted in increased hostility toward immigrants; as work became increasingly deskilled, no worker was irreplaceable, and no one's job was safe.

Nativist outbursts occurred in the Northeast from the 1830s to the 1850s, primarily in response to a surge of Irish Catholic immigration. In 1836, Samuel F. B. Morse ran unsuccessfully for mayor of New York City on a Nativist ticket, receiving only 1,496 votes. Following the Philadelphia Nativist Riots in the spring and summer of 1844, the Order of United Americans, a nativist fraternity, was founded in New York City.

The Development of Mormonism

Mormonism is the principal branch of the Latter Day Saint religious and cultural movement. The movement began with the visions of Joseph Smith, Jr. in the "Burned-over District" of upstate New York, which was so-called for the intense flames of religious revival that swept across the region.

Smith emphasized the importance of families being ruled by fathers. His vision of a reinvigorated patriarchy resonated with men and women who had not thrived during the market revolution, and his claims attracted those who hoped for a better future. Smith's new church placed great stress on work and discipline. He aimed to create a New Jerusalem where the church exercised oversight of its members.

American Renaissance

American Renaissance refers to a period of American literature from the 1830s to the end of the Civil War. The movement developed out of efforts by various American writers to formulate a distinctly American literature influenced by great works of European literature. Yet these novels, poems, and short stories utilized native dialect, history, landscape, and characters in order to explore uniquely American issues of the time, such as abolitionism, temperance, religious tolerance, scientific progress, the expanding western frontier, and the Native American situation.

Transcendentalism

Transcendentalism was America's first notable intellectual and philosophical movement. It developed in the 1830s and 1840s in the New England region of the United States as a protest to the general state of culture and society. Transcendentalism became a movement of writers and philosophers who were loosely bound together by adherence to an idealistic system of thought based on the belief in the essential supremacy of insight over logic and experience for the revelation of the deepest truths. Among the transcendentalists' core beliefs was the inherent goodness of both man and nature. Transcendentalists believed that society and its institutions—particularly organized religion and political parties—ultimately corrupted the purity of the individual. They had faith that man is at his best when truly "self-reliant" and independent. It was believed that only from such real individuals could true community be formed. Its fundamental belief was in the unity and immanence of God in the world.

The American Transcendentalists advocated the development of a national culture and efforts at humanitarian social reform, as well as debate on such issues as the abolition of slavery, womens' suffrage, workers' rights, educational innovation, and freedom of religion. The magazine *The Dial*, founded in 1840 by Margaret Fuller and Ralph Waldo Emerson, served as a forum for the publication of fiction, poetry, and essays by leading American Transcendentalists and writers of the American Renaissance.

Activating

Group Presentation

Religion and material has always been put on opposite position. After learning the whole lesson, especially the content of the Second Great Awakening, how do you deal with the material-religion problem? Choose your own starting point.

Exercising

✎ Compare and contrast the First Great Awakening and Second Great Awakening. (500—800 words)

_____

_____
_____
_____
_____
_____
_____
_____
_____

✎ Creative Writing:

Choose one of the themes below and imagine you were living in antebellum period. You can write in any genre you prefer: novel, poem, drama, etc. (1,500 words at least)

Subject 1: Women rights

Subject 2: Transcendentalism

Subject 3: Abolitionism

_____

_____
_____
_____
_____

Antebellum Culture Unit Eight

Homework

✐ Domestically, the uprising of real American literature helped build American culture and national image. Then what actions would America take in regard to foreign policy? What attitude would America hold concerning diplomacy?

✐ Choose your favorite figure included in this lesson and prepare a speech on him/her.

Unit Nine

Territory Expansion and Section Tension

1845	Texas annexation
1848	Treaty of Guadalupe Hidalgo ended the Mexican-American War
1850	Compromise of 1850
1851—1852	Publication of *Uncle Tom's Cabin*, by Harriet Beecher Stowe
1854	Beginning of "Bleeding Kansas"
1856	The beating of Senator Charles Sumner
1857	Dred Scott v. Sanford decision
1859	John Brown's raid on Harper's Ferry arsenal

Warming Up

1. Imagine you were a military colonel after Market Revolution and were pro-expansionist. What lands or nations would be your targets? Draw a map and paint your targets red. Please discuss your map about territory expansion with your classmates.
2. Read the plots from *Gone with the Wind* and talk about your feelings. What is the relationship like between South and North? What do you think caused such tensions?

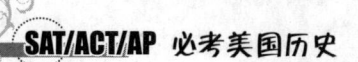

Mr. O'Hara: We've borne enough insults from the meddling Yankees. It's time we made them understand we'll keep our slaves with or without their approval. Who's to stop them right from the state of Georgia to secede from the Union!

Man: That's right!

Mr. O'Hara: The South must assert herself by force of arms.

Historical Highlights

Manifest Destiny

Manifest Destiny is a 19th century doctrine that the westward expansion of the United States to include the entire continent was inevitable and, most importantly, consistent with the God's will. It is first mentioned by John O'Sullivan in a newspaper discussing annexation of Texas.

Annexation of Texas

After Texas, a big slave colony, won independence from Mexico and wanted to join the United States, the annexation of Texas become a key issue in the 1844 presidential election due to the sectional tension. Many leaders of both major political parties opposed the idea of adding another huge slave state to a nation that was already beginning to experience an existential crisis regarding the issue of slavery. They also feared a war with Mexico. James K. Polk's vow to obtain both Texas and Oregon helped him win a decisive electoral victory. Since Polk, the pro-annexation Democrat, won the presidency, he promoted Texas Annexation and Texas joined the United States as the fifteenth slave state in 1845.

Mexican War

The annexation of Texas was the catalyst for the Mexican War. Both Mexico and United States had disputes over the border of Texas, and the Mexican War (1846—1848) began. The United States had many advantages, such as larger population and stronger navy, and won the war. In 1848, Mexico government signed the Treaty of Guadalupe Hidalgo, giving up its disputes about border and selling provinces of New Mexico and California.

California Gold Rush

As workers at John Sutter's sawmill found flecks of gold in the American River,

California in early 1848, a mass migration known as California Gold Rush began. People left home and went to California to pursue easy, quick riches. Only a very few actually "struck gold" and over time, finding even small amounts required expensive outlays and individual prospectors became fewer and fewer.

> Guiding Question: What might be the consequences of the California Gold Rush?

Gadsden Purchase

In the Gadsden Purchase of 1853, the United States obtained from Mexico another 29,670 square miles in southern Arizona and New Mexico. This purchase would facilitate a railroad across the continent.

Border Dispute with Great Britain

The United States and Great Britain had a dispute in 1842 over the border between Maine and British-ruled North American Colonies (Canada). Disputes over Minnesota territory also appeared between America and Canada after the Webster-Ashburton Treaty.

Fifty-Four Forty or Fight

Although British and United States agreed on a joint occupation of the Oregon Country, politicians pushed for U.S. ownership of Oregon. It is at 54°40' which the northern boundary locates. In this movement, "Fifty-Four Forty or Fight" was the call among those who wanted the whole ownership of the Oregon. Finally, Great Britain gave up all the territory and America established the border at 49th parallel.

Compromise of 1850

As California Gold Rush brought huge amounts of people, California's government drafted a constitution and asked to join the Union as a free state in 1849. This movement triggered the tension between the North and South. At this time, Henry Clay, the "Great Pacificator" stood out and proposed a series of measures to solve this contentious problem. These measures were later called the Compromise of 1850. The most significant proposal was that Congress admitted California as a free state but also enacted a stricter fugitive slave law. Popular sovereignty would decide the slavery issue in the New Mexico and Utah territories.

Sectionalism

The new Fugitive Slave Act was the intensification of the Compromise of 1850. Many northerners grew alarmed at this enforcement of catching slaves and many northern states passed personal liberty laws offering protection to fugitives. Also, northern states' protest,

Uncle Tom's Cabin—a book written by antislavery Harriet Beecher Stowe to detail the cruelty of slavery—increased the tension. The tension was intensified by President Franklin Pierce's Kansas-Nebraska Act, which divided the Nebraska Territory into Kansas and Nebraska and gave each territory the right to decide whether or not to become a slave territory. These three actions inflamed sectionalism hugely.

Party Realignment

In the 1840s, American politics increasingly centered on regional tensions, especially over the issue of slavery. The Whig Party disintegrated and became two parties—pro-slavery Democrats and antislavery Republicans. Also, some new political parties attempted to fulfill national parties' position. The Know-Nothing Party, evolving from anti-Catholic and anti-Irish movement, emerged in the 1840s. They opposed immigration. In 1854, the Republican Party was born. Opposition to slavery was the center of the Republican philosophy. It attracted many different people such as Whigs, Free-soilers and anti-slavery Democrats.

The Impending Crisis

After 1856, compromise on slavery was almost impossible and tensions between South and North led to violence. The three most significant events are Bleeding Kansas, the Dred Scott v. Sanford Decision, and John Brown's Raid. Bleeding Kansas was the 1854—1856 violence between pro-slavery and anti-slavery supporters in Kansas. The second event was about an African American slave, Dred Scott, who was taken north of the Missouri Compromise Line where slavery was banned. He argued that since he had lived several years in a free state, he should be deemed free. However, the Supreme Court stated that temporary residence in a free state didn't make Scott free. This decision reflected how slaves were considered as property, not human. The decision pleased southern people while angered northern people. The third event is John Brown's Rain. By the fall of 1859, Brown gathered 21 men to seize the federal armory at Harpers Ferry, Virginia. He hoped to send troops to slaves and foment a slave rebellion. Though the attempt failed, it gave South the impression that North would use violence to resolve their conflicts.

The Election of 1860

There were four major candidates in this election. Abraham Lincoln represented the Republican party, while Stephan A. Douglas and John C. Breckenridge were Democrats. The Constitutional Unionists were represented by John Bell. The election focused heavily on states rights, sovereignty and slavery in the territories, with Lincoln being opposed to adding

Territory Expansion and Section Tension Unit Nine

any new slave states. Perhaps aided by the fracturing of the Electoral College among his three rivals, Lincoln won the election.

> Guiding Question: How did this election contribute to the civil war?

Activating

1. Speech

What are the real reasons behind the outbreak of the Civil War?

2. Court imitation

Background: Supreme Court case—case of Dred Scott

Involved roles: 2 judges (summarize the case, state reasons and make decisions), 2 lawyers for either side (defend their side), 1 journalist (report the case from the beginning to the end)

Requirements: In the case of Dred Scott, you need to serve the leading positions in the Court and try to present the real conditions at the time to the utmost. The task contains debates and speeches.

Exercising

✍ Compare and contrast the different characteristics between northern territory and southern territory. (500—800 words)

_____

_____
_____
_____
_____
_____
_____
_____
_____
_____
_____

✎ It's said that Abraham Lincoln greeted Harriet Beecher Stowe in 1862 by saying "So you're the little woman who wrote the book that started this great war." So how do you understand this greeting? (500—800 words)

_____

_____
_____
_____
_____
_____
_____
_____
_____
_____
_____

Homework

✎ Create a drama about the Compromise of 1850. The students should form their own group. Be sure that the real conflicts in the meeting of 1850 are presented clearly (The drama itself contains debate and speech).

✎ Is America the only nation that took expansion actions at the time? Compare and contrast people's opinions about America's and another country's territory expansion in history. (You can choose Britain, France, etc.)

✎ Suppose you were a member of Republicans or Democrats, choose your own way to propaganda your party. You can create strong slogans, draw poster, make a speech, etc. The main political stand of either party must be included inside.

Unit Ten

Civil War and Reconstruction Era

1860	Election of President Abraham Lincoln
	South Carolina seceded from the United States and joined Confederacy
1861	Inauguration of Lincoln
	Six more states, all from the Deep South, seceded
	Fighting at Fort Sumter
	Four more states, from the upper South, seceded
	First Confiscation Act
1862	Homestead Act
	Morrill Land-Grant Acts
	Second Confiscation Act
1863	The Emancipation Proclamation went into effect
1863—1877	Reconstruction Era
1864	Sherman's March to the Sea
1865	Freedmen's Bureau was established
	Thirteenth Amendment was ratified
	Abraham Lincoln was assassinated
	Southern states began to pass Black Codes

1866	Civil Rights Act of 1866
	Ku Klux Klan was formed
	Ex parte Milligan
1867	Reconstruction Acts was passed
	Beginning of Congressional Reconstruction
	Tenure of Office Act
1868	President Andrew Johnson was impeached
	Fourteenth Amendment was ratified
1870	Fifteenth Amendment was ratified
1875	Civil Rights Act of 1875
1876	Beginning of Great Sioux War
	Disputed election between Samuel J. Tilden (Democrat) and Rutherford B. Hayes (Republican)
1877	Agreement ended Reconstruction
	Rutherford B. Hayes became president

Warming Up

1. The movie *Lincoln*, directed by Steven Spielberg talks about Lincoln and the Civil War. Have you watched the movie? Do you know any anecdotes about Lincoln?

2. Here are many interesting "facts" about the period of that age. Please decide whether these statements are true or not.

—Civil war was to eliminate monarchy.

—Lincoln's own children fought in the war.

—France and Britain both joined the civil war.

—Slavery triggered the conflict between northern and southern.

—Lincoln was a proponent of war.

Historical Highlights

Before the Civil War

Background of the Civil War

In the mid-19th century, while the United States was experiencing an era of tremendous growth, a fundamental economic difference existed between the country's northern and southern regions. While in the North, manufacturing and industry was well established, and agriculture was mostly limited to small-scale farms, the South's economy was based on a system of large-scale farming that depended on the labor of black slaves to grow certain crops, especially cotton and tobacco.

War Without Declaration

In the spring of 1861, decades of simmering tensions between the northern and southern United States over issues including states' rights versus federal authority, westward expansion and slavery exploded into the American Civil War (1861—1865). The election of the anti-slavery Republican Abraham Lincoln as president in 1860 caused seven southern states to secede from the Union to form the Confederate States of America; four more joined them after the first shots of the Civil War were fired.

During the War

The war itself began hesitantly, but after the Battle of Bull Run (Manassas) in July 1861, it was clear that warfare would last for many months, perhaps even years. Huge battles raged in places such as Fredericksburg, Chickamauga and Shiloh and in Virginia and Tennessee, where 40% of the 10,000 engagements of the war were fought. Winning victory after victory over poorly-led Union forces, Confederate General Robert E. Lee invaded Maryland in September 1862. But there he suffered a major loss at the Battle of Antietam, the bloodiest engagement of the war. The following year, Lee trounced the Union Army at Chancellorsville and invaded Pennsylvania, leading to the climactic Battle of Gettysburg in which 50,000 men were killed or wounded and Lee was forced to retreat to Virginia, never to invade the North again.

In the West, Union General Ulysses S. Grant took the important Confederate town of Vicksburg on the Mississippi River on 4 July 1863, the same day that news of the Union victory at Gettysburg reached Washington. Despite these key victories, the war was still not over. Grant launched his Overland Campaign in 1864 and fought a series of major battles. He hoped to destroy Lee's army by utilizing a strategy of attrition, but the tactic failed. Union General William Tecumsah Sherman marched from Atlanta to Savannah, burning the countryside as he went. By the spring of 1865, the South was exhausted, and on April 9, Lee surrendered to Grant at Appomattox Court House, effectively ending the war.

After the War

Emancipation Proclamation

Lincoln used the occasion of the Union victory at Antietam to issue a preliminary Emancipation Proclamation, which freed all slaves in the rebellious states after January 1, 1863.

Republicans During the Civil War

Generally belligerent toward the South, the Republicans were regarded by Southerners with a mix of hatred and fear as sectional tension increased. They were successful in the elections of 1858 and passed over their better-known leaders to nominate Abraham Lincoln in 1860. The party platform in 1860 included planks calling for a high protective tariff, free homesteads, and a transcontinental railroad; these were bids for support among Westerners, farmers, and eastern manufacturing interests.

Civil Liberties in Wartime

The Bill of Rights is intended to protect American citizens and American states.

But during Civil War period, the federal government, for the sake of power, intentionally undermined civil liberties defined in The Bill of Rights. This included the suspension of habeas corpus and freedom of speech.

Reconstruction
Wartime Reconstruction

After the war, the federal government pursued a program of political, social, and economic restructuring across the South—including an attempt to accord legal equality and political power to former slaves.

Reconstruction became a struggle over the meaning of freedom, with former slaves, former slaveholders and Northerners adopting different definitions. Eventually, faced with increasing opposition by white Southerners and some Northerners, the government abandoned efforts for black equality in favor of sectional reconciliation between whites.

Andrew Johnson

A Democrat, he championed populist measures and supported states' rights. During the U.S. Civil War (1861—1865), Johnson was the only Southern senator to remain loyal to the Union. Six weeks after Johnson was inaugurated as U.S. vice president in 1865, Lincoln was murdered. As president, Johnson took a moderate approach to restoring the South to the Union, and clashed with Radical Republicans. In 1868, he was impeached by Congress, but he was not removed from office. He did not run for a second presidential term.

Conflict Between Andrew Johnson and the Congress

Before Abraham Lincoln was assassinated in 1865, he had formulated a plan of reconstruction that would be lenient toward the defeated South as it rejoined the Union. He planned to grant a general amnesty to those who pledged an oath of loyalty to the United States and agreed to obey all federal laws pertaining to slavery (though high-ranking Confederate officials and military leaders were to be excluded from the general amnesty).

Lincoln's plan also stated that when a tenth of the voters who had taken part in the 1860 election had agreed to the oath within a particular state, then that state could formulate a new government and start sending representatives to Congress.

Andrew Johnson was intent on carrying out this plan when he assumed the presidency. This policy, however, did not sit well with the so-called Radical Republicans in Congress, who wanted to set up military governments and implement more stringent terms for readmission for the seceded states. As neither side was willing to compromise, a clash of wills ensued.

The political backing to begin impeachment proceedings against the president came when Johnson breached the Tenure of Office Act by removing Edwin Stanton, Secretary of War, from the cabinet. The Tenure of Office Act, passed over Johnson's veto in 1867, stated that a president could not dismiss appointed officials without the consent of Congress.

Both Lincoln and Johnson had experienced problems with Stanton, an ally of the Radicals in Congress. Stanton's removal, therefore, was not only a political decision made to relieve the discord between the president and his cabinet, but a test of the Tenure of Office Act as well. Johnson believed the Tenure of Office Act was unconstitutional and wanted it to be legally tried in the courts. It was the president, himself, however, who was brought to trial.

President Johnson was impeached by the House of Representatives on February 24, 1868 and the Senate tried the case in a trial that lasted from March to May 1868. In the end, the Senate voted to acquit President Andrew Johnson by a margin of 35 guilty to 19 not guilty—one vote short of the two-thirds needed to convict.

Black Codes

Under the lenient Reconstruction policies of President Andrew Johnson, white southerners reestablished civil authority in the former Confederate states in 1865 and 1866. They enacted a series of restrictive laws known as "black codes", which were designed to restrict freed blacks' activity and ensure their availability as a labor force now that slavery had been abolished. For instance, many states required blacks to sign yearly labor contracts; if they refused, they risked being arrested as vagrants and fined or forced into unpaid labor.

13th, 14th, 15th Amendments

The Thirteenth Amendment to the United States Constitution officially abolished and continues to prohibit slavery to this day.

The Fourteenth Amendment to the United States Constitution declared that all persons born or naturalized in the United States are American citizens including African Americans.

The Fifteenth Amendment to the United States Constitution prohibits each government in the United States from denying a citizen the right to vote based on that citizen's race, color, or previous condition of servitude.

Civil Rights Act of 1875

The Civil Rights Act of 1875 was introduced to Congress by Charles Sumner and Benjamin Butler in 1870 but did not become law until 1st March, 1875. It promised that all persons, regardless of race, color, or previous condition, was entitled to full and equal employment of accommodation in "inns, public conveyances on land or water, theaters, and other places of public amusement." In 1883 the Supreme Court declared the act as unconstitutional and asserted that Congress did not have the power to regulate the conduct and transactions of individuals.

Practice of Reconstruction
Scalawags and Carpetbaggers

During and immediately after the Civil War, many northerners headed to the southern states, driven by hopes of economic gain, a desire to work on behalf of the newly emancipated slaves or a combination of both. These "carpetbaggers"—whom many in the South viewed as opportunists looking to exploit and profit from the region's misfortunes—supported the Republican Party, and would play a central role in shaping new southern governments during Reconstruction. In addition to carpetbaggers and freed African Americans, the majority of Republican support in the South came from white southerners who for various reasons saw more of an advantage in backing the policies of Reconstruction than in opposing them. Critics referred derisively to these southerners as "scalawags."

Sharecropping

With the southern economy in disarray after the abolition of slavery and the devastation of the Civil War, conflict arose between many white landowners attempting to reestablish a labor force and freed blacks seeking economic independence and autonomy. Many former slaves expected the federal government to give them a certain amount of land as compensation for all the work they had done during the slavery era. Union General William T. Sherman had encouraged this expectation in early 1865 by granting a number of freed men 40 acres each of the abandoned land left in the wake of his army. During Reconstruction, however, the conflict over labor resulted in the sharecropping system, in which black families would rent small plots of land in return for a portion of their crop, to be given to the landowner at the end of each year.

End of Reconstruction

After 1867, an increasing number of southern whites turned to violence in response to the revolutionary changes of Radical Reconstruction. The Ku Klux Klan and other white supremacist organizations targeted local Republican leaders, white and black, and other African Americans who challenged white authority. Though federal legislation passed during the administration of President Ulysses S. Grant in 1871 took aim at the Klan and others who attempted to interfere with black suffrage and other political rights, white supremacy gradually reasserted its hold on the South after the early 1870s as support for Reconstruction waned. Racism was still a potent force in both South and North, and Republicans became more conservative and less egalitarian as the decade continued. In 1874—after an economic depression plunged much of the South into poverty—the Democratic Party won control of the House of Representatives for the first time since the Civil War.

When Democrats waged a campaign of violence to take control of Mississippi in 1875, Grant refused to send federal troops, marking the end of federal support for Reconstruction-era state governments in the South. By 1876, only Florida, Louisiana and South Carolina were still in Republican hands. In the contested presidential election that year, Republican candidate Rutherford B. Hayes reached a compromise with Democrats in Congress: In exchange for certification of his election, he acknowledged Democratic control of the entire South. The Compromise of 1877 marked the end of Reconstruction as a distinct period, but the struggle to deal with the revolution ushered in by slavery's eradication would continue in the South and elsewhere long after that date. A century later, the legacy of Reconstruction would be revived during the civil rights movement of the 1960s, as African Americans fought for the political, economic and social equality that had long been denied them.

Activating

1. Debate

Please have a debate over the topic: whether Lincoln was a racist. (Researching on his personal life is very helpful.)

2. Debate

Please have a debate over the topic: Was the Civil War successful or not? You need to outline the consequences, problems and changes occurring after the Civil War.

Exercising

An essay topic: Will American citizens still have a civil war, if Lincoln didn't win the election of 1860? (800—1000 words)

Civil War and Reconstruction Era Unit Ten

_____
_____
_____
_____
_____
_____
_____

✍ Please make a chart to outline the strengths and weaknesses of northern and southern respectively.

	Strengths	Weaknesses
South		
North		

Homework

✍ Write a letter to your family as a southern soldier or a northern one who fights on the frontier of the Civil War.

You can get more information about the life of soldiers on this website:

http://www.historynet.com/civil-war-soldiers

✍ If you are the person who is responsible for building the tomb of Lincoln, what will you write for his epitaph?

✍ The southern government is offering you a seat in the Military Strategy Conference. Please write a report to guide the southern to win the victory.

As an American history learner, you have known that South's failure is doomed. But wars are complicated and triumph of a war is linked to several elements. So use your imagination and senses to prepare South for Civil War.

101

✍ Use your own language with your drawings to illustrate your understanding towards the 13th, 14th, 15th amendments.

✍ Do some research on Andrew Johnson. You are required to have a speech expressing your comments on him.

Unit Eleven

South and West During Reconstruction

1863—1877	Reconstruction Era
1866	Civil Rights Act of 1866
	Ku Klux Klan was formed
	Ex parte Milligan
1867	Medicine Lodge Treaty establishes the reservation system
	Reconstruction Acts was passed
	Tenure of Office Act
1868	President Andrew Johnson was impeached
	Fourteenth Amendment was ratified
1870	Fifteenth Amendment was ratified
1875	Civil Rights Act of 1875
1876	Disputed election between Samuel J. Tilden (Democrat) and Rutherford B. Hayes (Republican)
1877	Agreement ended Reconstruction
	Rutherford B. Hayes became president

Warming Up

1. When Obama won the president election of 2008, there was a popular sentiment that this was the real end to Civil War. How do you understand this opinion? Is it true or not?

2. Nowadays, racial discrimination is still a severe problem throughout the world, including America. What do you think causes such a problem?

3. Suppose you were a Native American living in the west during the Reconstruction Era. Can you imagine what kind of life you would lead?

Historical Highlights

Racial Segregation in the New South

Jim Crow Laws

A series of segregation laws were passed in the southern states in the years after Reconstruction came to an end. These laws came to be known as Jim Crow laws. The origins of the term can perhaps be attributed to a song-and-dance routine from the 1830s called "Jump Jim Crow," which included white actors in blackface caricaturing African Americans. Later in the century, "Jim Crow" became a pejorative term for African Americans. The laws applied to African Americans, therefore, became known as Jim Crow laws. They relegated African-Americans to second-class status in the South.

Jim Crow laws continued in force until 1965. They mandated racial segregation in all public facilities in states of the former Confederate States of America, starting in 1890 with a *"separate but equal"* status for African Americans. Facilities for African Americans were consistently inferior and underfunded compared to those available to European Americans. This body of law institutionalized a number of economic, educational, and social disadvantages. The laws segregated public facilities, such as railroad cars, bathrooms, restaurants, and schools. Segregation mainly applied to the Southern states, while Northern segregation was generally de facto—patterns of housing segregation enforced by private covenants, bank lending practices, and job discrimination, including discriminatory labor union practices.

Plessy v. Ferguson

In 1890, the state of Louisiana passed the Separate Car Act that required separate accommodations for blacks and whites on railroads. Classified as black, Plessy bought a first-class ticket at the Press Street Depot and boarded a "whites only" car of the East Louisiana Railroad in New Orleans, Louisiana. John Howard Ferguson, the judge, ruled that Louisiana had the right to regulate railroad companies while they operated within state boundaries. Plessy was convicted and sentenced to pay a $25 fine.

African Americans in Politics

The Fifteenth Amendment to the U.S. Constitution gave the vote to all male citizens regardless of color or previous condition of servitude. African Americans became involved in the political process not only as voters but also as governmental representatives at the local, state and national level. Although their elections were often contested by whites, and members of the legislative bodies were usually reluctant to receive them, many African American men ably served their country during Reconstruction. Most famous are Senator Hiram R. Revels and Representatives Benjamin S. Turner, Josiah T. Walls, Joseph H. Rainey, Robert Brown Elliot, Robert D. De Large, and Jefferson H. Long.

Conflicts in the New West

Homestead Act

Signed into law in May 1862, the Homestead Act opened up settlement in the western United States, allowing any American, including freed slaves, to put in a claim for up to 160 free acres of federal land. By the end of the Civil War, 15,000 homestead claims had been established, and more followed in the postwar years. Eventually, 1.6 million individual claims would be approved; nearly ten percent of all government held property for a total of 420,000 square miles of territory.

End of Native Americans' Autonomy

When large number of immigrants poured into America, the American government wanted to explore westwards. The United States government undertook negotiations with the Native American Plains tribes living between the Arkansas and Missouri rivers to ensure protected right-of-way for the migrants. The signing of Treaty of Laramie (1851) marked the government's intervention again into Native Americans tribes and the end of Native Americans' autonomy.

Treaty of Laramie (1851)

Many Indians have referred to the treaty as the Horse Creek Treaty. The United States Senate ratified the treaty, adding Article 5, to adjust compensation from fifty to ten years, if the tribes accepted the changes. Acceptance from all tribes, with the exception of the Crow, was procured. But several tribes never received the commodities promised as payments. The treaty produced a brief period of peace, but it was broken by the failure of the United States to prevent the mass emigration of miners and settlers. Such emigrants competed with the tribal nations for game and water, straining limited resources and resulting in conflicts with the emigrants. The U.S. government did not enforce the treaty to keep out the emigrants.

The Great Sioux Uprising of 1862

The Great Sioux uprising of 1862 was an armed conflict between the United States and eastern "Sioux". Throughout the late 1850s, treaty violations by the United States and late or unfair annuity payments by Indian agents caused increasing hunger and hardship among the Dakota. A council of Dakota decided to attack settlements throughout the Minnesota River valley to try to drive whites out of the area. There has never been an official report on the number of settlers killed, although in Abraham Lincoln's second annual address, he noted that not less than 800 men, women, and children had died.

The Sand Creek Massacre (1864)

In the second half of 19th century, the discovery of gold brought a tremendous influx of white men seeking fortunes, infringing on the buffalo hunting grounds and territories of the Native Indians. Leaders of tribes sought peaceful solutions to the white-man invasion at first. But tensions were still rising in 1864. Leaders held a meeting with white men and believed a peaceful resolution had been made. After the meeting, they set up camp at Sand Creek, an area that had been promised to be a safe zone for the Indians. However, on the morning of November 29, 1864, Chivington and his men launched their assault on Sand Creek. The attack left some 200 Cheyenne men, women, and children dead.

Reservation System

Under the reservation system, American Indians kept their citizenship in their sovereign tribes, but life was harder than it had been. The reservations were devised to encourage the Indians to live within clearly defined zones, and the U.S. promised to provide food, goods and money and to protect them from attack by other tribes and white settlers. The reservation policy also reflected the views of some of the educators and protestant missionaries that forcing the Indians to live in a confined space with little opportunity for nomadic hunting would make it easier to "civilize the savages."

Native Indians, after 1830, found themselves being confined to reservations. But, even the Indian Territory was not safe from white settlers. In 1854, the Federal Government abolished the northern half of Indian Territory and established the Kansas and Nebraska Territories, which were immediately opened up to white settlement. Many of the tribes occupying the land ended up on vastly reduced reservations.

The Dawes Act

The Dawes Act of 1887 was adopted by Congress in 1887, authorizing the President of the United States to survey American Indian tribal land and divide it into allotments for individual Indians. Those who accepted allotments and lived separately from the tribe would be granted United States citizenship. The objectives of the Dawes Act were to lift the Native Americans out of poverty and to stimulate assimilation of them into mainstream American society. Individual household ownership of land and subsistence farming on the European-American model was seen as an essential step. Government sold extra lands on the open market, allowing purchase and settlement by non-Native Americans.

The Ghost Dance Movement

The Ghost Dance was a new religious movement incorporated into numerous American Indian belief systems. According to the teachings of the Northern Paiute spiritual leader Wovoka (renamed Jack Wilson), proper practice of the dance would reunite the living with spirits of the dead, bring the spirits of the dead to fight on their behalf, make the white colonists leave, and bring peace, prosperity, and unity to Indian peoples throughout the region. The Ghost Dance was associated with Wilson's (Wovoka's) prophecy of an end to white expansion while preaching goals of clean living, an honest life, and cross-cultural cooperation by Indians. Practice of the Ghost Dance movement was believed to have contributed to Lakota resistance to assimilation under the Dawes Act.

Activating

1. Speech

Form a Congress with 4—5 members. Now there is a resolution on encroaching on the west and robbing the lands of Native American tribes. Everyone in the Congress should voice his stance and give a speech on the reasons behind his decision.

2. Debate

During the Reconstruction Era, "Separate but Equal" slogan is popular and widely-accepted. Divide into two groups and debate on the legitimacy of "Separate but Equal".

Exercising

✍ Assess the possible effects of racial segregation. (500—800 words)

_____

_____
_____
_____
_____
_____
_____
_____
_____

✍ If Lincoln had not been assassinated, what would have happened in Reconstruction Era? Would history be changed? (500—800 words)

South and West During Reconstruction — Unit Eleven

Homework

✐ Suppose you were a Native American in the west. You wrote diaries every day. Try writing your diary of one day. In your diary you should realistically record your routine, feeling and other content you think suitable.

✐ Literature and arts have always been a way for humans to release their pressure, emotions and, even deeper, inside suffering. Suppose you were a Southern black man, what was your situation? Try expressing it in your own way. You can choose any genre you like. (dances, songs, dramas, psalm, etc.)

*Tip: the genre you choose should fit the era. For example, if you want to write an academic report, you need to take into consideration black men's average literacy.

Unit Twelve

Gilded Age

1869	Founding of the Knights of Labor
1873	Panic of 1873
1876	Alexander Graham Bell developed the telephone
	Custer's Last Stand
1877	Great Railroad Strike
	Munn v. Illinois
1879	Thomas A. Edison developed the light bulb
1881	Helen Hunt Jackson published *A Century of Dishonor*
1882	Formation of the Standard Oil Trust
	Chinese Exclusion Act
1883	Opening of the Brooklyn Bridge
1886	Founding of the American Federation of Labor
	Haymarket bombing
	Wabash, St. Louis and Pacific Railway Company v. Illinois
1887	Interstate Commerce Act

	Opening of the first subway system in the United States (Boston)
	Dawes Severalty Act
1889—1991	Ghost Dance movement
1890	Sherman Antitrust Act
	Massacre at Wounded Knee
1892	Homestead lockout
1893	World's Columbian Exposition (Chicago World's Fair)
	Panic of 1893
1894	Pullman strike
1895	United States v. E.C. Knight Company
1896	Plessy v. Ferguson

Warming Up

1. Have you even seen the novel *Gilded Age* from Mark Twain? If you saw it before, please give a summary of the book.
2. How do you understand the meaning of "Gilded Age"? Do you think it was a really flourishing period or seemingly flourishing period?

Historical Highlights

The Robber Barons

As corporations, a form of group joint and legal ownership of companies, developed, they tried to maximize their profits in several ways, including integration and monopoly. Gradually, both consumers and the federal government came to view the power of the corporations as unfair and inappropriate. People therefore called the men who controlled major industries and cheated their consumers "Robber Barons". Famous among these were Andrew Carnegie (steel industry), John D. Rockefeller (oil exploration), John Pierpont Morgan (J. P. Morgan Company, banking and finance) and Cornelius Vanderbilt (railroad, steamboats).

Attitudes Toward Business

Government policies encouraged the success of business in late 1800s. The government at that time enacted protective tariffs and encouraged laissez-faire policies, which allowed little government intervention in corporations. However, as critics of corporate power grew in number, the government started to examine company regulation. Two Supreme Court cases are Wabash, ST. L. &. P. RY. CO. v. State of Illinois and United States vs. E. C. Knight Company. In response to these critics, the theory of Social Darwinism appeared. It said that the inequalities of wealth were part of the process of survival of the fittest.

The Rise of Organized Labor

Although industrialization brought general improvements to American society, workers often struggled to survive. Under worsening working conditions and for low pay, workers started to be alarmed at these insults to their sense of pride and ability to control the conditions of work space. They responded by forming and joining labor organizations.

Labor Strikes

Several violent strikes happened during the 1870s through the 1890s as labor unions rose and expanded. The first major strike occurred in the Railway industry in 1877, responding to wage cuts, from the Baltimore and Ohio Railroad, causing massive property destruction in nine states. The second one, the Haymarket Square Riot, caused by people's desire of eight-hour workday. After police stepped in, strikers and police came to fight. This event made employers worried about labor unions. The third strike, the Homestead Strike of 1892, occurred after a union refused to accept pay cuts, and local police and militia came in to suppress the unrest. After they lost the strike, steelworker unions lost power throughout the country. The fourth strike, the Pullman Strike of 1894 was cause by a 25% reduction in wages without reducing rents or price of groceries at company store. Railroad workers around country refused to handle Pullman cars. Finally, president Cleveland sent troops to end the unrest. As a result, the court upheld an injunction saying that the government could prevent disruption of interstate commerce and delivery of the mail.

Democrats and Republicans

Neither of these two parties took strong stands on most of the issues of the Gilded Age, except tariffs. Democrats wanted lower tariffs rates while Republicans wanted higher tariff rates. Both parties took more care of big business. Owners of big companies supported congressmen with contributions, gifts and outright bribery. So, corruption was a significant part of American political life during the Gilded Period.

The Election of 1876 and Presidency of Rutherford B. Hayes

At first, neither Democratic candidate Samuel Tilden nor Republican candidate Rutherford B. Hayes could clearly claim victory, because 20 electoral votes were disputed. To resolve this deadlock, the parties agreed to the Compromise of 1877. This agreement gave Hayes the presidency, essentially in exchange for withdrawing Union/Federal troops from the south, ending the period of Reconstruction. This left the South essentially free to return to pre-Civil War policies, and led directly to expansion and abuse of the Jim Crow Laws mentioned before.

The Election of 1880 and the Assassination of President Garfield

James A. Garfield, a Republican, won the presidency of 1880 but was shot six months after his inauguration in 1881. After his assassination by a mentally unstable man who believed Garfield owed him a political debt.

The Presidency of Cleveland

The Democratic candidate, Grover Cleveland, advocated lowering tariffs and consequently, he won the election of 1884. He also signed the law—Interstate Commerce Commission which challenged the power of big business. He is the only U.S. president to serve non-consecutive terms, from 1885—1889 and 1893—1897.

The Presidency of Chester Arthur

Chester Arthur, the president after Garfield, signed the Pendleton Act into the law. The Pendleton Act let the President decided which jobs would be filled by a Civil Service Commission. People would then compete for jobs by taking exams. Chester Arthur also tackled the problem of tariffs into the consideration.

The Harrison Presidency

Benjamin Harrison won the presidential election of 1888. During his presidency, he signed the McKinley Tariff (1890) which was the highest in the history and kept many foreign goods out of the country. This angered many people. He also signed the Sherman Antitrust Act (1890) which outlawed trusts that interfered with interstate trade.

The Panic of 1893 and the Currency Issue

In 1893, the vigorous economic growth came to a halt. Several railroad companies went bankrupt and many people lost jobs. Peoples' faith in the government was shaken. Many scholars thought that one major cause was an inadequate amount of currency in circulation. In 1873, Congress only allowed for the coinage of gold which was beneficial for businessman while harmful to the poor. As the economy grew in the Gilded Age period, the money didn't have the ability to grow.

Farmers Challenge the Two-Party System

Suffering from the high fees of railroad companies and a small supply of currency, farmers tried to seek solutions through political action. The Greenback Party was formed in 1874 and called for issuing paper money that was not backed on silver or gold. A farmers' organization—The Grange—was established and called for state laws to protect farmers' interests. In many Midwestern states, they were successful in passing laws that regulated railroad freight rates. Formed in 1892, The Populist Party called for moving away from the gold standard in favor or unlimited silver-coinage.

The Election of 1896 and the "Cross of Gold" Speech

The Election of 1896 helped establish the identity of the major political parties in the twentieth century. The major problem in this election was the amount of currency in circulation. The Republican candidate—William McKinley, a decidedly pro-business candidate, encouraged sticking to the gold standard. The Democratic candidate—William Jennings Bryan, the more pro-egalitarian candidate gave a speech called "Cross of Gold" and favored "free and unlimited coinage of silver".

Activating

1. Speech

If you were the leader of workers' strikes, try to give a sensational speech to encourage your cause.

2. Debate

Do you think that Gilded Age has a positive or negative influence on America's overall history? Use facts to support your debate.

Exercising

✎ If you were a Republican or Democrat, write about your opinion about tariff issues. Would you increase or lower it?

_____

_____
_____
_____
_____
_____
_____
_____
_____
_____
_____

Homework

✎ Discuss: How do policies apply to the ideology of other fields (for example, Social Darwinism)?

✎ Creative Writing: Write a novel about Gilded Age. You can imitate Mark Twain's novel.

Unit Thirteen

Cross-Continental Expansion

1893	Queen Liliuokalani was toppled by a coalition of U.S. marines and businessmen
1898	Spanish-American War
	United States annexation of Hawaii
	Formation of the American Anti-Imperialist League
	Treaty of Paris
1899—1900	Secretary of State John Hay established the Open Door policy in China
1899—1902	Philippine-American War
1900	Hurricane and flood in Galveston, Texas
1901	Publication of *The Octopus: A California Story*, by Frank Norris
1903	The United States acquired the Panama Canal Zone (Canal completed, 1914)
	Elkins Act
1904	Publication of *The Shame of the Cities*, by Lincoln Steffens
	Publication of *The History of the Standard Oil Company*, by Ida Tarbell
	Election of Theodore Roosevelt
1905	Founding of the Niagara Movement
1906	Theodore Roosevelt won the Noble Peace Prize
	Publication of *The Jungle*, by Upton Sinclair
	Meat Inspection Act
	Passage of the Pure Food and Drug Act
	Hepburn Act

Historical Highlights

Reasons for Overseas Imperialism

The United States entered the overseas imperialism scramble a little after the major European powers began carving up Africa and Asia. Many Americans resisted the idea of the United States embarking on overseas expansion; after all, the United States was born in a war against a major imperial power. However, several factors led United States political leaders to engage in overseas expansion.

Imperialism vs. Colonialism

The two terms are not always interchangeable. Colonialism usually implies the effort of one country to establish a settlement in another land; imperialism usually implies the effort to rule territory that is already occupied.

Alfred Thayer Mahan and *the Importance of Naval Power*

Alfred Thayer Mahan stressed the importance of naval power in achieving and maintaining influence on the world stage. This idea might seem commonplace, but the United States throughout the nineteenth century was more focused on domestic issues and expansion over the American continent. He pushed for the United States to develop a strong navy, maintain military bases and coaling stations throughout the world, and administer an overseas empire. These ideas were central to his book, *The Influence of Sea Power Upon History, 1660—1783* (1890).

Industrialization and the Depression of 1893

Contributing to the push for imperialism was the unprecedented growth of American industry. Some policy makers thought that imperialism would become necessary if the United States were to become the world's predominant industrial power. Imperial holdings would provide American industry with important raw materials. Also, the people in these new American possessions could provide a market for the growing output of consumer products that American industry was turning out. The desire for new markets intensified with the onset of the panic of 1893. This economic downturn left Americans unable to absorb additional consumer items. The economy did not begin to improve until 1896.

"The White Man's Burden"

Imperialist ventures were motivated by a particular cultural set of ideas that created a racial hierarchy. Mainstream thinking in the United States in the late 1800s posited the superiority of the descendants of the Anglo-Saxon people, and the inferiority of the non-white peoples of the world. This racist notion was widely held, but it led to divergent impulses. Some white Americans felt it was the duty of the "civilized" peoples of the world to uplift the less fortunate; others felt that the inferior races would simply disappear in a struggle for the "survival of the fittest." The push to uplift the peoples of the world was made clear in Rudyard Kipling's famous poem, "The White Man's Burden" (1899). Josiah Strong, a Protestant clergyman, echoed Kipling's sentiment. He argued that the "Anglo-Saxon" race had a responsibility to "civilize and Christianize" the world.

The racial hierarchy implicit in "The White Man's Burden" was starkly displayed at the World's Fair in Chicago in 1893, as a sideshow of the "exotic" people's of the world was presented to attendees. These displays of "natives" were contrasted with the industry and progress of the advanced civilizations. The obvious implication was that the advances of civilization must be made available to the rest of the world. Frederick Douglass attended the fair and, with Ida B. Wells, wrote a scathing critique of the racist assumptions of the fair, and it is important to recognize that the notions mentioned above ideas were not universally accepted. In regard to both slavery and white supremacy, important voices challenged the mainstream thinking of the day.

Christian Missionaries

Christian missionary work went hand-in-hand with American expansion. Missionaries were eager to spread the Christian gospel and introduce new populations to Christianity. Many of these missionaries targeted China's large population.

Hawaii

American missionaries arrived in Hawaii as early as the 1820s. Later in the century, American businessmen established massive sugar plantations, undermining the local economy. Discord between the American businessmen and the ruler of the island, Queen Liliuokalani, emerged after 1891. The pineapple grower Sanford Dole urged the United States to intervene. American businessmen staged a coup in 1893, toppling Queen Liliuokalani. U.S. forces immediately protected a new provisional government, led by Dole. The provisional government hoped for U.S. annexation of the islands, but that did not occur until 1898.

The Spanish-American War and Its Aftermath

The Spanish-American War was a turning point in terms of America's role in the world beyond North America. As a result of the war, the United States acquired island territories, became more involved in the Caribbean and Latin America, acquired the Philippines after a protracted struggle, and became increasingly involved in Asia.

United States Interest in Cuba

In the 1890s, Spain was still in control of Cuba, but a Cuban independence movement was trying to break its ties to Spain. The Spanish governor of Cuba, Valeriano Weyler, used brutal tactics to suppress the rebellion. Thousands of Cubans were crowded into concentration camps. By 1898, approximately a quarter of Cuba's rural population (approximately 300,000 people) had died as a result of starvation and disease. Many Americans wanted the United States to intervene on Cuba's side in its struggle against Spanish rule. Some Americans saw parallels between the Cuban struggle for independence from Spain and America's struggle for independence from Great Britain. Also, some American businessmen were angered by the interruption of the sugar harvest by the fighting between Cuban rebels and Spanish forces.

"Yellow Journalism" and the Call to War

Events in Cuba were brought to the attention of ordinary Americans through mass-produced and mass-distributed newspapers. Industrialization and increased literacy set the groundwork for America's first mass media. To attract customers, newspapers began printing bold, sensational headlines, often disregarding accepted journalistic practices and even the truth. This sensational journalism came to known as "yellow journalism." News organizations used these techniques of exaggeration and innuendo to build support for war with Spain. These newspapers breathlessly followed events in Cuba, with lurid accounts of Spanish wrongdoing and condemnations of "Butcher" Weyler—the Spanish governor.

The Sinking of the Maine

The event that led directly to the Spanish-American War was the destruction of a United States warship, the USS *Maine*, in the harbor of Havana, Cuba. Many in the United States thought that the destruction of the ship was the work of Spain, especially after American newspapers bluntly accused Spain of the crime, despite the scarcity of evidence.

The Spanish-American War

The Spanish-American War was brief. American forces landed in Cuba on June 22, 1898, and Spain surrendered on July 17. Fighting in the Philippines—also held by Spain—lasted just days, as Admiral George Dewey led American forces in taking the capital city of Manila. Theodore Roosevelt led a charge up San Juan Hill in a key battle for Cuba. The colorful Roosevelt and his men— known as the "Rough Riders"—made headlines in American papers, and elevated Roosevelt's status in the political realm.

The Treaty of Paris

The United States and Spain negotiated the Treaty of Paris (1898) following the war. In the treaty, Spain agreed to cede the Philippines, Puerto Rico, and Guam to the United States; the United States agreed to pay Spain $20 million for these possessions.

Cuba and the Platt Amendment

Cuba gained its independence following the Spanish American War, but in many ways, Cuba became independent in name only. The United States wanted to ensure that American economic interests would not be challenged by a future Cuban administration. The United States, therefore, insisted that the Platt Amendment be inserted into the Cuban Constitution. This amendment allowed the United States to militarily intervene in Cuban affairs if it saw fit. The amendment limited the Cuban government's ability to conduct its foreign policy and to manage its debts. Also, the amendment allowed the United States to lease a naval base at Guantanamo Bay. Americans troops intervened in Cuba three times between 1902 and 1920.

Debate over the Role of the United States Globally

As America became increasingly involved in world affairs, debates ensued in the United States about the country's proper role. These debates pitted imperialists against anti-imperialists and, later, interventionists against isolationists.

Imperialism and National Identity

As the dust settled following the Spanish-American War, the American public realized that the Treaty of Paris would grant the United States ongoing control of several lands beyond America's existing borders. The United States had recently annexed Hawaii (1898). The Treaty of Paris (1898) would give the United States control over Puerto Rico, Guam, and the Philippines. Although Cuba was technically independent, the Platt Amendment made it a U.S. protectorate. To many Americans, these acquisitions were markedly different from earlier acquisitions; these new islands were densely populated and were far away from the settled parts of the United States, unlike the Louisiana Purchase (1803) or the Mexican Cession (1848). Perhaps the distinction amounted to splitting hairs, but critics did surmise one additional key difference. The earlier territorial gains of the United States were intended to absorb American citizens and to eventually achieve statehood and equal footing with the existing states. There was no expectation, on the other hand, that the Philippines would absorb large numbers of American citizens. The United States would, indefinitely, rule *over* a foreign population, much as Great Britain had ruled over the Thirteen Colonies.

The American Anti-Imperialist League

In 1898, as the Treaty of Paris was debated in the Senate, a group of critics of American imperialism formed the American Anti-Imperialist League. The league was a coalition of conservative Democrats (known at the time as "Bourbon Democrats") as well as more progressive elements. The league included the American author Mark Twain, who became increasingly radical as he grew older. He was the vice president of the league from 1901 to 1910, and wrote some of the league's more scathing condemnations of imperialism.

The league suffered a major schism in 1900, as the more conservative members rejected the candidacy of Democrat William Jennings Bryan, while the more progressive elements embraced it. Jennings was an anti-imperialist, but many of his other positions, especially his criticism of the gold standard, alienated many of the conservative "Bourbon Democrats." The Republican William McKinley won reelection, continuing an aggressive foreign policy. The debate over whether the United States Constitution permitted the American government to make rules for peoples who were not represented by lawmakers nearly stopped the ratification of the Treaty of Paris. Democratic opponents of imperialism rallied against the treaty, which barely achieved the necessary two-thirds majority in 1899.

Does the Constitution Follow the Flag?

The question of whether Constitutional provisions applied to people in the new American territories continued in the courts after the ratification of the Treaty of Paris. Expansionists argued that the Constitution did not necessarily follow the flag; anti-imperialists insisted that it should. The Supreme Court settled this issue in a series of cases in 1901 that have come to be known as the Insular cases ("insular" means island-related). The Court agreed with expansionists that democracy and imperialism are not incompatible, and that the imperial power need not grant its colonial subjects constitutional rights. The decisions were based on the racist assumption that the colonial subjects were of an inferior race, and the colonial power had the responsibility to uplift these peoples before granting them autonomy.

War in the Philippines

Many Filipinos were surprised and disappointed to learn that the United States decided to hold on to the Philippines as a colony after the Spanish-American War. They had seen the United States as a liberating force that would help rid the nation of Spanish rule and usher in independence. This was not the intent of the United States. Following the ratification of the Treaty of Paris, a bitter, three-year-long war, known as the Philippine-American War, ensued that was far more lengthy and deadly than the Spanish-American War itself (Filipino forces continued to resist American control for another decade). Filipino forces were led by Emilio Aguinaldo. The war cost American forces 4,000 lives. Estimates vary in regard to the number of Filipino casualties; historians estimate 20,000 to 30,000 Filipinos died in the conflict and perhaps another 200,000 (and possibly more) civilians died. The United States held on to the Philippines until after World War II (1946).

A Tale of Two Wars

In writing about American imperialism, don't forget about the war in the Philippines. It lasted longer (three years) and resulted in more casualties (more than 4,000 American deaths; possibly 200,000 or more Filipino deaths) than the better known Spanish-American War (four months; fewer than 400 American deaths; fewer than 15,000 combined Cuban and Spanish deaths).

China and the Open Door Policy

The bitter conflict in the Philippines was in many ways designed to provide the United States a stepping-stone to an even greater prize—trade with China. China's large population and natural resources made it a target for the imperialist nations. The major powers of Europe had previously begun carving up China. Britain, Japan, Germany, Russia, and France each proclaimed a "sphere of influence"—a port city and surrounding territory—in which other foreign nations would be excluded. The United States asserted that all of China should be open to trade with all nations. The United States secretary of state, John Hay, wrote a series of notes to the major powers asserting an "open door" policy for China. The United States claimed to be concerned for the territorial integrity of China, but was more interested in gaining a foothold in trade with China. The "open door" policy was begrudgingly accepted by the major powers.

The Boxer Rebellion

Christian missionaries had come to China in large numbers, but met with little success there. The number of converts was small, and the presence of the missionaries inspired militant anti-foreign secret societies. The most well known of these societies was the Boxers, or the Society of Righteous and Harmonious Fists. The Boxers led a rebellion that resulted in the death of more than 30,000 Chinese converts as well as 250 foreign nuns. The United States participated in a multination force to rescue westerners held hostage by the Boxers (1900).

Theodore Roosevelt and the "Big Stick"

In September 1901, President McKinley was shot at the Pan-American Exposition in Buffalo, New York, by the anarchist Leon Czolgosz and soon died from the wound, just six months into his second term as president. His vice president, Theodore Roosevelt, became president. Roosevelt was an adventurer, an expansionist, and a hero of the Spanish-American War. His foreign policy approach is neatly summed up in his famous adage that the United States should "speak softly, but carry a big stick" when dealing with other nations (Roosevelt had borrowed the phrase from an African proverb). The "big stick" implied the threat of military force. He envisioned the United States acting as the world's policeman, punishing wrongdoers. He asserted that the "civilized nations" had a duty to police the "backward" countries of the world. He claimed that the United States had the right to militarily intervene in the nations of Latin America. This assertion of American might is known as the Roosevelt Corollary to the Monroe Doctrine. In 1902, he sternly warned Germany to stay out of the Americas after Venezuela failed to repay a loan to Germany and Germany threatened military intervention.

Foreign Policy and Economic Priorities

Often in American history, economic priorities drive foreign policy decisions. A Central American canal was a major priority for American commercial and industrial interests at the beginning of the twentieth century.

Panama and the Panama Canal

Roosevelt's aggressive approach to Latin America is clearly evident in regard to Panama. With the acquisition of Pacific territories and with an increased interest in trade with China, American policy-makers became interested in a shortcut to the Pacific. Merchant ships and naval ships had to travel around the southern tip of South America to reach the Pacific Ocean. The building of a canal through Panama, therefore, became a major goal of Roosevelt. Before 1903 Panama was a region of Columbia. American investors picked the narrow piece of land as an ideal location for a canal to facilitate shipping between the Atlantic and Pacific Oceans. When Columbia refused the U.S. offer of $10 million to build a canal, American investors, with the backing of President Roosevelt and the United States military, instigated a "rebellion" in Panama against Columbia. Panama became an independent country and immediately reached a deal with the United States to build a canal. President Roosevelt boasted that he "took Panama."

Roosevelt, Diplomacy, and the Nobel Peace Prize

President Roosevelt was interested in establishing the United States as a major player in world diplomacy. Toward this end, he acted as a mediator between France and Germany in their conflict over Morocco (1905). Roosevelt was also interested in maintaining a balance of power among the other world powers. That same year, Roosevelt offered to mediate an end to the Russo-Japanese War (1904—1905). A peace conference was held in Portsmouth, New Hampshire, with Roosevelt presiding. Despite Roosevelt's aggressive actions in Latin America, he was granted the Nobel Peace Prize (1906) for his other diplomatic efforts.

The Nobel Prize

Three other United States presidents have won the Nobel Peace Prize: Woodrow Wilson in 1919; Jimmy Carter in 2002; and Barack Obama in 2009.

The "Gentleman's Agreement"

In 1907, the diplomatic gains that Roosevelt had achieved with Japan were threatened by discriminatory legislation passed in California, restricting the rights of "Orientals." Roosevelt quietly worked out a "Gentleman's Agreement" with Japan, in which Japan agreed to limit immigration to the United States and Roosevelt agreed to pressure officials in California to end discriminatory practices.

President Taft and "Dollar Diplomacy"

President William Howard Taft (1909—1913) continued to pursue an aggressive foreign policy, but he put more emphasis on expanding and securing American commercial interests than on pursuing the global strategic goals that Roosevelt had championed. Taft's foreign policy has come to be known as "Dollar Diplomacy." He sent troops to Nicaragua and the Dominican Republic to coerce them into signing commercial treaties with the United States. In general, he tried to substitute "dollars for bullets" in pursuing American interests. He failed to stem revolution in Mexico in 1911.

President Wilson's Foreign Policy

President Wilson's initial focus as president was on domestic concerns. However, his administration became increasingly drawn into foreign policy matters, from problems in the Americas to war in Europe. Wilson was driven by both a desire to secure American economic interests abroad and by a strong moral compass; often these impulses clashed with each other.

Lack of Volunteers

The tepid response to President Wilson's call to volunteer reflects the mixed feelings Americans had about the war. Wilson immediately signaled a break with his Republican predecessors by appointing the anti-imperialist William Jennings Bryan to be secretary of state. Bryan sought peaceful accommodations of differences with many nations, but he and Wilson were not above flexing America's military muscle in the Americas. Wilson authorized the occupation of Nicaragua by American marines to suppress a rebellion against the American-backed president of the country. He sent troops to Haiti in 1915 and to the Dominican Republic in 1916 to ensure that American business interests were not challenged.

Wilson and the Mexican Revolution

President Wilson became enmeshed in the convulsions of the Mexican Revolution, which lasted through the 1910s. The revolution began with the ousting of an autocratic leader in 1910. The revolution soon degenerated into a civil war that left nearly a million Mexicans dead. In 1914, Wilson challenged the legitimacy of the new Mexican leader, General Victoriano Huerta. He sent 800 marines to Mexico. Huerta fled the country, and a new government, more amenable to American interests, came to power. This new government was challenged by an uprising led by the rebel leader Francisco "Pancho" Villa. Villa successfully intercepted a train carrying American gold and led a raid into American territory that left eighteen Americans dead. Wilson authorized more than 12,000 troops to invade Mexico to capture Villa. Villa eluded the American forces, and the United States, in early 1917, began preparations for World War Ⅰ.

Activating

1. Debate

Do you think that the action of cross-continental is a good and necessary action?

2. Presentation

Collect data and reasons to make a group presentation. Topic: Why the imperialism occurred at that time throughout the world?

Cross-Continental Expansion Unit Thirteen

Exercising

✍ Write an essay about the role yellow journalism played in the cross-continental expansion.

_____

_____
_____
_____
_____
_____
_____
_____
_____
_____
_____
_____

Homework

✍ Make a chart to describe the influence about the American cross-continental expansion on the world patterns.

Example:

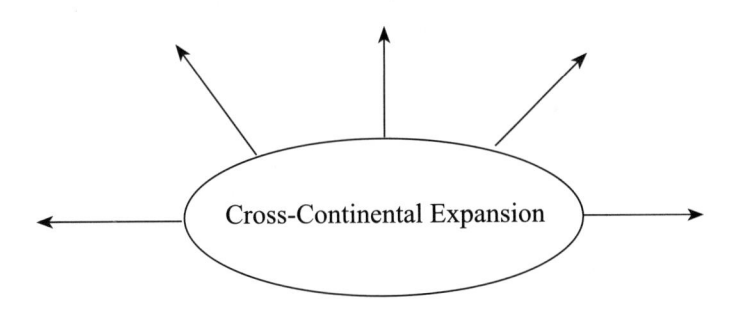

(Cross-Continental Expansion)

✍ Search and compare imperialism in different countries (i.e. Britain, Italy, Germany…) and try to personate each country with a specific animal and explain the reason.

127

Unit Fourteen

Progressive Movement

1908	Election of William Howard Taft
1909	Creation of the National Association for the Advancement of Colored People
	Mann Act
1912	Election of Woodrow Wilson
1913	Sixteenth Amendment (federal income tax) was ratified
	Seventeenth Amendment (direct election of senators) was ratified
	Henry Ford introduced the conveyor belt to automobile production
	Federal Reserve Act
1914	Federal Trade Commission
	Clayton Antitrust Act
	Beginning of World War I

Warming Up

1. Would US citizens think they need to solve the issues in the country? What kind of issues did they have?
2. Have you read a novel called *The Jungle* which exposed serious flaws in the factories?

Historical Highlights

The Progressive Movement

The Progressive Movement was an effort to cure many of the ills of American society that had developed during the great spurt of industrial growth in the last quarter of the 19th century. The frontier had been tamed, great cities and businesses developed, and an overseas empire established, but not all citizens shared in the new wealth, prestige, and optimism.

Women in the Progressive Movement

Women activists, mainly from middle-class and prosperous social backgrounds, emphasized the special contribution that women could make in tackling these problems. With issues of public health and safety, child labor, and womens' work under dangerous conditions so prominent, who are better than women to address them? Focusing on issues that appealed to women as wives and mothers, and promoting the notion that women were particularly good at addressing such concerns, the female activists practiced what womens' historians call maternalist politics.

Pragmatism

Pragmatism as a philosophical tradition began in the United States around 1870. Charles Sanders Peirce, generally considered to be its founder, later described it in his pragmatic maxim: "Consider the practical effects of the objects of your conception. Then, your conception of those effects is the whole of your conception of the object." Pragmatism rejects the idea that the function of thought is to describe, represent, or mirror reality. Instead, pragmatists consider thought an instrument or tool for prediction, problem solving and action.

Progressive Movement Unit Fourteen

Muckrakers

The muckrakers provided detailed, accurate journalistic accounts of the political and economic corruption and social hardships caused by the power of big business in a rapidly industrializing United States. The name muckraker was a pejorative when used by U.S. President Theodore Roosevelt in his speech of April 14, 1906.

The Jungle

The Jungle, by Upton Sinclair, is full of graphic descriptions of the meat-packing industry. The lines were so moving and troubling that the novel inspired the establishment of the Food and Drug Administration (FDA).

Muller v. Oregon

In *Muller v. State of Oregon*, the U.S. Supreme Court ruled that the governmental interest in protecting womens' procreative value outweighed the "right" of women to have free contracts, and upheld an Oregon law limiting the hours that women employed in factories and laundries could work. The *Muller* ruling—that the governmental interest in protecting social welfare outweighed the freedom of contract—set the stage for later New Deal protections, culminating in the gender-neutral Fair Labor Standards Act of 1938.

Theodore Roosevelt

The rising young Republican politician Theodore Roosevelt unexpectedly became the 26th president of the United States in September 1901, after the assassination of William McKinley. Young and physically robust, he brought a new energy to the White House, and won a second term on his own merits in 1904. Roosevelt confronted the bitter struggle between management and labor head-on and became known as the great "trust buster" for his strenuous efforts to break up industrial combinations under the Sherman Antitrust Act. He was also a dedicated conservationist, setting aside some 200 million acres for national forests, reserves and wildlife refuges during his presidency. In the foreign policy arena, Roosevelt won a Nobel Peace Prize for his negotiations to end the Russo-Japanese War and spearheaded the beginning of construction on the Panama Canal. After leaving the White House and going on safari in Africa, he returned to politics in 1912, mounting a failed run for president at the head of a new Progressive Party.

Woodrow Wilson

Woodrow Wilson (1856—1924), the 28th U.S. president, served in office from 1913 to 1921 and led America through World War I (1914—1918). An advocate for democracy and world peace, Wilson is often ranked by historians as one of the nation's greatest presidents. Wilson was a college professor, university president and Democratic governor of New Jersey before winning the White House in 1912. Once in office, he pursued an ambitious agenda of progressive reform that included the establishment of the Federal Reserve and Federal Trade Commission. Wilson tried to keep the United States neutral during World War I but ultimately called on Congress to declare war on Germany in 1917. After the war, he helped negotiate a peace treaty that included a plan for the League of Nations. Although the Senate rejected U.S. membership in the League, Wilson received the Nobel Prize for his peacemaking efforts.

Activating

1. Presentation

Please divide into 4 groups to give a sensational presentation. Each group would present as one of the four kinds of people: women, African Americans, workers and middle class. In order to represent them, you might need to know their wages, living conditions, goals and dissatisfactions.

2. Debate

Set a debate over the Progressive Movement from the poor's and the rich's perspectives respectively. Is Progressive Movement effective or not?

Exercising

Essay: How successful were progressive reforms during the period 1890—1915 with respect to two of the following: industrial condition and urban life politics?

Progressive Movement — Unit Fourteen

Homework

- Compare and contrast Darwinism in the Progressive Movement period and in the Gilded Age.
- Make a chart to show policies which each state published. One column should be the name of the state and the other one should be the brief knowledge of the policies.
- Draw a caricature from one of the perspectives of women, African Americans, workers or middle class to show real living conditions.
- Write a short passage showing your understanding towards progressive movement.

Unit Fifteen

World War I

1914	Beginning of World War I
1914—1917	United States intervention in Mexico
1915	Release of D.W. Griffith's film: *The Birth of a Nation*
1916	Reelection of Woodrow Wilson
1917	Espionage Act
1918	Sedition Act Armistice ended World War I

Warming Up

1. Here are several countries for your consideration: Britain, France, Russia, Swiss, America, Italy, and Austria-Hungary. Choose a country and draft their foreign policy in 1914—1920. (Which countries do you think will be enemies and which one will you collaborate with?)
2. World War I broke out in 1914. Based on what you learnt, how would it influence America?

Historical Highlights

The World at War

World War I was a vast conflict that included all the major powers of the Europe and overseas allies. The immediate provocation was a relatively minor incident—the assassinations of the heir to the Austro-Hungarian Empire—but the causes were long-standing and much more complex. Usually, nationalism, imperialism, militarism and the alliance system are considered the long-standing causes. After the assignation, Austria-Hungary allied with Germany declared war on Allied Powers which included Russia, France and Great Britain.

The United States Neutrality

During the first three years of the war, the United States kept neutral in the war. American public opposed participate in a European war. Also, neutrality allowed America to trade with both sides and gave loans to allies.

From Neutrality to Intervention

Although America wanted to remain neutral during the war, several events had caused it toward intervention. Some short causes are trade, public opinions, Wilson's speech, the sinking of the *Lusitania* and Zimmerman Telegram. Great Britain had blockaded Germany, so trade shifted to Britain. Public opinion also shifted to the Allied Powers due to wartime news coverage which tended to describe Germany as "beasts" and Britain as "civilized". President Wilson's attitude changed from neutrality to joining the war after his reelection. Additionally, the sinking of British ocean liner *Lusitania* and the Zimmerman Telegram from Germany which proposed an alliance with Mexico against America in exchange for lands they had lost to the United States angered most of the Americans. Finally, the last straw for America was the sinking of hundreds of American ships by German submarine attacks. In April 1917, United States declared war.

The United States at War

The government passed the Selective Service Act (1917) to organize a draft of American men in the wartime. Also, African-American troops were organized into the 92nd Division and fought side by side with French troops for over six months. After long-time fighting, the

German army surrendered on November 11, 1918 and ended World War I.

The War at Home and Civil Rights Limitations

America's participation in war impacted the home front a lot. President Wilson expanded government power and limited civil liberty. The Espionage Act (1917) and the Sedition Act (1918) made it illegal to interfere with the draft or with the sale of war bonds as well as say anything against the war. The Supreme Court also stated that the government is justified in limiting certain forms of speech during wartime in the case of *Schenck v. United States (1919)*. Besides several acts, the government formed federal agencies like The War Industries Board to help the war.

The War at Home—Women Suffrage

The war also brought substantial social changes. It gave women new chances and the right to vote. Many women moved into workforce during the war because most of the young men went to the battlefields. They formed the National Woman's Party in 1917. Finally, women convinced President Wilson to support their suffrage demands. In 1919, Congress passed the Nineteenth Amendment giving women rights to vote.

The War at Home—African Americans

The war was an opportunity for African Americans to show their loyalty and patriotism. They fought a lot in the battlefields. Meanwhile, a great movement from the rural south to the industrial north was taking place. This movement was later called The Great Migration. They left south for several reasons. Some hoped to escape the unequal treatment in the south. Others wanted to get better jobs and improved economic situations.

The Postwar World—Wilson's Fourteen Points

President Wilson was determined to shape the structure of the postwar world. He wanted "peace without victory". Therefore, he posted the Fourteen Points (1918) which promoted freedom of seas, removal of trade barriers, reduction of Armaments and creation of League of Nations. However, only the creation of League of Nations is agreed by European countries. Although Wilson posted Fourteen Points, the Congress rejected the Treaty of Versailles and the United States didn't join the League of Nations.

Postwar Society—Flu, Strike and Red Scare

Participation in WWI derailed domestic reform efforts and created a conservative backlash. Returning soldiers brought the Spanish Flu to America and caused lots of death.

After the war, federal agencies dismissed and inflation was no longer kept in check by the government. In 1919, the price rose nearly 75 percent. Fighting to protect wartime gains, more than 4 million workers went on strike at one time or another. The reaction against labor was partly spurred by a wave of fear of radicals and communists, which called the Red Scare. The emergence of the Soviet Union as a communist nation fed these fears. People feared radicals and communist revolution in the United States. In December 1919, Russian-born activist Emma Goldman was deported. In January 1920, Attorney General A. Mitchell Palmer began a broad hunt for suspected radicals, later called the Palmer raids.

Activating

1. Speech

If you were an African American or a woman in WWI, how would you declare your social position?

2. Debate

Should civil rights be limited during WWI?

Exercising

✍ Do you think it is inevitable for America to enter WWI?

✎ Assess the influence of WWI on America from at least three perspectives.

_____

_____
_____
_____
_____
_____
_____
_____
_____
_____

Homework

✎ Write a letter: You are a German in America during WWI and you are going to write a letter to your family in Germany to describe what your life is like during WWI.

✎ Write a national song for America. It should be suitable for war condition.

✎ Make a set of introduction cards about important countries during WWI. Each card should include not only basic information on these countries, but also their military conditions.

Unit Sixteen

America after WWI

1919	Eighteenth Amendment (prohibition) was ratified
	Creation of the Comintern
	Deportation of Emma Goldman
	Schenck v. United States
	Seattle General Strike
1919—1920	Boston Police Strike
1920	Nineteenth Amendment (women's right to vote) was ratified
	Height of the "Palmer raids"
	Election of Warren G. Harding
1921	Emergency Quota Act
	Beginning of the Teapot Dome Scandal
1924	National Origins Act
	Election of Calvin Coolidge
1925	Scopes trial
1927	Execution of Sacco and Vanzetti
1928	Kellogg-Briand Pact
	Election of Herbert Hoover
1929	Stock market crash

Warming Up

1. Hollywood was a small community in 1870 and was incorporated as a municipality in 1903. It officially merged with the city of Los Angeles in 1910, and soon thereafter a prominent film industry began to emerge, eventually becoming the most recognizable film industry in the world.

2. The "**Lost Generation**" was the generation that came of age during World War I. The term was popularized by Ernest Hemingway, who used it as one of two contrasting epigraphs for his novel, *The Sun Also Rises*. In that volume Hemingway credits the phrase to Gertrude Stein, who was then his mentor and patron. This generation included artists and writers who came of age during the war such as F. Scott Fitzgerald, T. S. Eliot, James Joyce, Sherwood Anderson, John Dos Passos, John Steinbeck, William Faulkner, Djuna Barnes, Waldo Peirce, Isadora Duncan, Abraham Walkowitz, Ezra Pound, Alan Seeger, Franz Kafka, Henry Miller, Aldous Huxley, Malcolm Cowley, Louis-Ferdinand Céline, Erich Maria Remarque and the composers Sergei Prokofiev, Paul Hindemith, George Gershwin, and Aaron Copland.

3. If you are a German immigrant, describe your response under the situation after WWI.

Historical Highlights

Anti-Immigrant Sentiment

Nativism, or opposition to immigration, rose sharply in the years after World War I.

A large wave of immigrants from southern and eastern Europe had arrived in the United States between 1880 and 1920. There are several reasons nativists resented this new wave of immigration. Some nativists focused on the fact that most of the new immigrants were not Protestant. Poles and Italians tended to be Catholic, Russians and Greeks tended to be Eastern Orthodox, and Jews came from several countries in eastern Europe. The cacophony of languages heard on the streets of New York or Chicago repelled many nativists. Some Americans were anti-European after the trauma of World War I. Some nativists associated immigrants with either radical movements or drunkenness. Finally, working-class people feared that low-wage immigrant laborers would take jobs from native-born American workers.

The Quota System

The nativist sentiment that characterized the postwar period led to passage of legislation that greatly reduced the number of immigrants allowed into the United States. The Emergency Quota Act (1921) and the National Origins Act (1924) set quotas for new immigrants based on nationality. The first act set the quota for each nationality at 3 percent of the total number of that nationality that was present in the United States in 1910. The second act reduced the percentage to 2 percent and moved the year back to 1890. This had the effect of setting very low quotas for many of the "new immigrants"—from eastern and southern Europe.

The Trial of Sacco and Vanzetti

The repressive atmosphere of the Red Scare era can be seen in the trial of Nicola Sacco and Bartolomeo Vanzetti. Their trial for robbery and murder illustrated the intolerance that many Americans had toward immigrants and radicals in the 1920s. The two men were accused of robbing and killing a payroll clerk in Massachusetts in 1920. The evidence against them was sketchy but the judge was openly hostile to the two men, who were not only immigrants but also anarchists. After they were found guilty, many Americans protested the verdict and wondered if an immigrant, especially with radical ideas, could get a fair trial in the United States. Despite protests the two men were executed in 1927.

The Resurgence of the Ku Klux Klan

The original Ku Klux Klan, a violent, racist group with its roots in the immediate aftermath of the Civil War, had died out by the 1870s. By the 1920s, however, the organization was a genuine mass movement. By 1925, it grew to 3 million members, by its own estimate. The Klan was devoted to white supremacy and "100 percent Americanism."

Rural and Urban Responses to Prohibition

The movement to ban alcohol from American society was one of the largest movements in the nineteenth and early twentieth centuries. It finally achieved success in 1919 when prohibition became national policy with the ratification of the Eighteenth Amendment to the Constitution. The amendment called for a ban on the manufacture, sale, and transportation of alcoholic beverages. However, the victory of the movement proved to be hollow. Although per capita consumption of alcohol dropped dramatically in the early 1920s, it increased as the decade progressed, possibly approaching pre-Prohibition levels by 1925. Further, the amount of lawlessness in America went up as bootleggers, speakeasies, and organized crime filled the gap left by the death of the legitimate alcoholic beverage industry. Criminal activity became so widespread that Congress ratified the Twenty-first Amendment (1933), which repealed Prohibition.

The Bible Versus Science

During the 1920s, a large number of Americans, especially in the South, adopted a fundamentalist, literal approach to the Bible and to religion. The Scopes trial of 1925 illustrated the conflict between Protestant fundamentalism and modern science. The Scopes trial involved the teaching of evolution in public schools. John Scopes, a Tennessee biology teacher, was arrested for violating the Butler Act, a state law forbidding the teaching of evolution. The case turned into a national spectacle, with the famous lawyer Clarence Darrow representing Scopes and William Jennings Bryan representing the state. It is one of several important events that highlighted cultural divisions in the 1920s.

The Impact of New Technology

Technological advances in the first decades of the twentieth century improved standards of living, increased personal mobility, and created better systems of communications.

Radio and the Development of Mass Culture

Radio grew from being virtually nonexistent at the beginning of the 1920s to becoming an extremely popular medium by the end of it. The medium was begun by amateurs who sent out music or sermons to the few scattered people who had "wireless receivers." Soon, Westinghouse and other corporations saw the potential to reach the masses with radio. By 1923, there were almost 600 licensed radio stations. Early successful programs included *The Amos 'n' Andy Show* (1928), a holdover from "blackface" minstrel shows of the nineteenth century.

The Rise of the Motion Picture Industry

Movie attendance achieved staggering levels in the 1920s. By the end of the decade, three-fourths of the American people (roughly 90 million) were going to the movies every week. The first "talkie," *The Jazz Singer*, came out in 1927.

The Harlem Renaissance

The Great Migration of African Americans from the rural South to the urban North contributed to the Harlem Renaissance, a literary, artistic, and intellectual movement centered in the African-American neighborhood of Harlem, in New York City. A key goal of the movement was to increase pride in African-American culture by celebrating African-American life and forging a new cultural identity among African-American people. Contributions included the poetry of Langston Hughes, Claude McKay, and Countee Cullen and the jazz music of Louis Armstrong, Duke Ellington, and Bessie Smith. Langston Hughes's poems include "Harlem," "The Negro Speaks of Rivers," and "I, Too, Sing America." He wrote an essay that became a manifesto for Harlem Renaissance writers and artists entitled "The Negro Artist and the Racial Mountain." Duke Ellington is perhaps the most important figure in twentieth century jazz. Some of his most important compositions are "Mood Indigo," "Don't Get Around Much Anymore," and "Take the A Train."

The "Lost Generation" Writers of the 1920s

The "Lost Generation" literary movement expressed a general disillusionment with society, commenting on everything from the narrowness of small town life to the rampant materialism of American society. Several writers were troubled by the destruction and seeming meaninglessness of World War I. *The Great Gatsby* (1925) by F. Scott Fitzgerald exposed the shallowness of the lives of the wealthy and privileged of the era. Sinclair Lewis's novels, such as *Main Street* (1920) and *Babbitt* (1922), mocked the narrowness of the middle class. Ernest Hemingway's *A Farewell to Arms* (1929) critiqued the glorification of war.

Henry Ford and Mass Production

The most important figure in the development of new production techniques was Henry Ford. In 1913 he opened a plant with a continuous conveyor belt. The belt moved the chassis of the car from worker to worker, so that each did a small task in the process of assembling the final product. This mass production technique reduced the price of his Model T car, and also dealt a blow to the skilled mechanics who had previously built automobiles. Unskilled assembly line workers gradually replaced skilled craft workers in American industry.

Scientific Management

An important aspect of mass production was the scientific management techniques developed by Frederick Winslow Taylor. Taylor carefully watched workers, noted the most efficient techniques, and wrote down in exacting detail how a particular task was to be done. Work became not only more efficient, but also more monotonous. Many workers, especially those with a degree of skill, resisted the loss of control and autonomy that scientific management techniques entailed.

Advertising and Mass Consumption

If the quality of work deteriorated for factory workers in the 1920s, the availability of consumer goods to average workers greatly increased. Cars, radios, toasters, health and beauty aids, and other consumer goods filled showrooms and stores. The advertising industry also changed a great deal in the 1920s. Advertising and public relations industry tapped into the ideas of Freudian psychology and crowd psychology. Many ads in this period attempted to reach the public on a subconscious level, rather than presenting products and services in a straightforward manner. The public relations pioneer Edward Bernays, a nephew of Sigmund Freud, was a key figure in the shift in marketing toward elaborate corporate advertising campaigns. Easy credit and layaway plans also helped move merchandise.

The Presidency of Warren Harding

Harding had been a newspaper publisher in Ohio before entering politics. He was handsome and well-liked among the Republican political cronies with whom he regularly played poker. His abilities as a leader, however, were less than presidential. When the Republican national convention of 1920 deadlocked, the party bosses decided "in a smoke-filled room" to deliver the nomination to Harding as a compromised choice.

Harding recognized his limitations and hoped to make up for them by appointing able men to his cabinet. He appointed the former presidential candidate and Supreme Court justice Charles Evans Hughes to be secretary of state; the greatly admired former mining engineer and Food Administration leader Herbert Hoover to be secretary of commerce; and the Pittsburgh industrialist and millionaire Andrew Mellon to be secretary of the treasury. When the Chief Justice's seat on the Supreme Court became vacant, Harding filled it by appointing former President William Howard Taft. The one surprise decision of Harding's presidency was his pardoning of Socialist leader Eugene Debs and winning his release from federal prison. (While a prisoner for violating the Espionage Act in wartime, Debs had nevertheless won 920,000 votes in the 1920 election as the Socialist candidate for president.) Harding's pardoning of Debs was prompted by the president's generous spirit—certainly not by ideology, since Harding was a conservative.

Harding's Domestic Policy

Harding did little more than sign into law the measures adopted by the Republican Congress. He approved (1) a reduction in the income tax, (2) an increase in tariff rates under the Fordney-McCumber Tariff Act of 1922, and (3) establishment of the Bureau of the Budget, with procedures for all government expenditures to be placed in a single budget for Congress to review and vote on.

Harding's Scandals and Death

Curiously, Harding's postwar presidency was marked by scandals and corruption similar to those that had occurred under an earlier postwar president, Ulysses S. Grant. Having appointed some excellent officials, Harding also selected a number of incompetent and dishonest men to fill important positions, including Secretary of the Interior Albert B. Fall and Attorney General Harry M. Daugherty. In 1924, Congress discovered that Fall had accepted bribes for granting oil leases near Teapot Dome, Wyoming. Daugherty also took bribes for agreeing not to prosecute certain criminal suspects. Shortly before these scandals were uncovered, however, Harding died suddenly in August 1923 while traveling in the West. He was never implicated in any of the scandals.

The Presidency of Calvin Coolidge

Harding's vice president and successor, Calvin Coolidge, had won popularity in 1919 as the Massachusetts governor who broke the Boston police strike. He was a man of few words who richly deserved the nickname "Silent Cal." Coolidge once explained why silence was good politics. "If you don't say anything," he said, "you won't be called on to repeat it." Also unanswerable was the president's sage comment: "When more and more people are thrown out of work, unemployment results." Coolidge summarized both his presidency and his era in the phrase: "The business of America is business."

The Election of 1924

After less than a year in office, Coolidge was the overwhelming choice of the Republican party as their presidential nominee in 1924. The Democrats nominated a conservative lawyer from West Virginia, John W. Davis, and tried to make an issue of the Teapot Dome scandal. Unhappy with conservative dominance of both parties, liberals formed a new Progressive party led by its presidential candidate, Robert La Follette of Wisconsin. Coolidge won the election easily, but the Progressive ticket did extremely well for a third party in a conservative era. La Follette received nearly 5 million votes, chiefly from discontented farmers and laborers.

Coolidge's Vetoes and Inaction

Coolidge believed in limited government that stood aside while business conducted its own affairs. Little was accomplished in the White House except keeping a close watch on the budget. Cutting spending to the bone, Coolidge vetoed even the acts of the Republican majority in Congress. He would not allow bonuses for World War I veterans and vetoed a bill (the McNary-Haugen Bill of 1928) to help farmers cope with falling crop prices.

The Politics of Isolationism in the 1920s

Isolationist sentiment ran high in the United States. Many Americans were disillusioned about World War I while others had grown resentful of the wave of "new immigrants" who had come to America. The United States remained outside the League of Nations (refer here for the rejection of the Treaty of Versailles).

Tariffs

Debates about tariff rates have existed throughout American history, from Alexander Hamilton's "Report on Manufactures" (1791) to the passage of the North America Free Trade Agreement (1994). Tariff rates were passionately debated in the nineteenth century.

Higher Tariff Rates

The isolationist Republican presidents of the 1920s enacted higher tariffs to keep out foreign goods. In 1922, the Fordney-McCumber Act dramatically raised tariff rates. In 1930, in the midst of the Great Depression, isolationist legislators pushed through the Smoot-Hawley Tariff Act, which increased tariffs to their second highest rate in United States history, exceeded only by the "Tariff of Abominations" (1828).

Tariffs in the 1920s

Tariffs in the 1920s were at their highest rate in American history other than in the period following the "Tariff of Abominations." Raising tariff rates during the 1920s was exactly what the country didn't need. The United States needed to trade more with Europe in order to sell excess goods. Tariffs closed off trade with Europe.

Washington Conference

The presidents of the 1920s attempted to isolate the United States from world affairs, and reduce spending on war munitions. President Harding successfully pressed for a reduction of naval power among Britain, France, Japan, Italy, and the United States at the Washington Disarmament Conference in 1921.

The Kellogg-Briand Pact

The United States was one of sixty-three nations to sign the Kellogg-Briand Pact, renouncing war in principle. The pact was unenforceable, negotiated outside of the League of Nations and, therefore, ultimately meaningless.

Activating

1. Drama
Each group choose one side from the veteran, African American, women group, middle class people, government authorities. And please hold a mimic meeting to discuss the funding and the needs after WWI.

2. Discussion
From the current situation, please discuss whether the United States attend to WWI is a wise choice.

3. Presentation
What do you think of the formation of the League of Nations?

Exercising

✎ Assess possible effects of conservation on American society.

_____

_____

_____

_____

Homework

- Based on the characteristic of the Hollywood at that time, please try to make a movie. (select your own theme)
- Write a fiction on the lost generation.
- Please write a song about the jazz music (with lyrics).
- Imagining you are the minister of the education department, what educational policies will you choose to release?

Unit Seventeen

Great Depression and New Deal

1929	Stock market crash
	The Great Depression began
1930	Hawley-Smoot Tariff
1932	Bonus March
	Reconstruction Finance Corporation was established
	Franklin D. Roosevelt was elected president
1933	The Marx Brothers' movie *Duck Soup* was released
	The 100 Days
	"Bank holiday"
	Agricultural Adjustment Act (AAA)
	Glass-Steagall Act (Federal Depositors Insurance Corporation was established)
	National Industrial Recovery Act (NIRA)
	Civilian Conservation Corps (CCC)
	Ratification of the Twenty-first Amendment (repeal of prohibition)
1934	Share Our Wealth clubs were started by Huey Long
	Securities and Exchange Commission
1935	Clifford Odets writes the play *Waiting for Lefty*

	National Labor Relations Act (Wagner Act)
	Social Security Act
	Schechter decision struck down NIRA
	Works Progress Administration
	First Neutrality Act
1936	Butler decision struck down the AAA
	Roosevelt was elected to a second term
	Charlie Chaplin's *Modern Times* was released
1936—1939	Spanish Civil War
1937	"Roosevelt Recession"
	Roosevelt's "court packing" plan
	Farm Security Administration
	Panay Incident & Quarantine Speech

Warming Up

1. What kind of issues do you think might appear at this time? Hint: There were some problems with the mass production in America. But why?

2. Can you recognize what is happening in the pictures?

Historical Highlights

Great Depression

The Great Depression (1929—1939) was the deepest and longest-lasting economic downturn in the history of the Western industrialized world. In the United States, the Great Depression began soon after the stock market crash of October 1929, which sent Wall Street into a panic and wiped out millions of investors. Over the next several years, consumer spending and investment dropped, causing steep declines in industrial output and rising levels of unemployment as failing companies laid off workers. By 1933, when the Great Depression reached its nadir, some 13 to 15 million Americans were unemployed and nearly half of the country's banks had failed. Though the relief and reform measures put into place by President Franklin D. Roosevelt helped lessen the worst effects of the Great Depression in the 1930s, the economy would not fully turn around until after 1939, when World War II kicked American industry into high gear.

Herbert Hoover

Herbert Hoover (1874—1964), America's 31st president, took office in 1929, the year the U.S. economy plummeted into the Great Depression. Although his predecessors' policies undoubtedly contributed to the crisis, which lasted over a decade, Hoover bore much of the blame in the minds of the American people. As the Depression deepened, Hoover failed to recognize the severity of the situation or leverage the power of the federal government to squarely address it.

Bank Crisis

Just days before Franklin D. Roosevelt's inauguration as President, the United States was in the middle of a banking panic. On March 3, 1933, Washington Governor Clarence Martin closed all Washington State banks and declared a three-day "bank holiday," working with other state governments to pushing for the passage of a federally mandated bank holiday. The banking system was unable to keep up with the panicked withdrawals that customers were making from their bank accounts, rendering banks incapable of providing money many customers had deposited.

Franklin D. Roosevelt

Franklin D. Roosevelt was in his second term as governor of New York when he was elected as the nation's 32nd president in 1932. With the country mired in the depths of the Great Depression, Roosevelt immediately acted to restore public confidence, proclaiming a bank holiday and speaking directly to the public in a series of radio broadcasts or "fireside chats." His ambitious slate of New Deal programs and reforms redefined the role of the federal government in the lives of Americans. Reelected by comfortable margins in 1936, 1940 and 1944, FDR led the United States from isolationism to victory over Nazi Germany and its allies in World War II. He spearheaded the successful wartime alliance between Britain, the Soviet Union and the United States and helped lay the groundwork for the post-war peace organization that would become the United Nations. The only American president in history to be elected four times, Roosevelt died in office in April 1945.

New Deal

By 1932, one of the bleakest years of the Great Depression, at least one-quarter of the American workforce was unemployed. When President Franklin Roosevelt took office in 1933, he acted swiftly to try and stabilize the economy and provide jobs and relief to those who were suffering. Over the next eight years, the government instituted a series of experimental projects and programs, known collectively as the New Deal, that aimed to restore some measure of dignity and prosperity to many Americans.

Marginal Workers

Undocumented and authorized immigrant laborers, female workers, workers of color, guest workers, and unionized workers together compose an enormous and diverse part of the labor force in America. Labor and employment laws are supposed to protect employees from various workplace threats, such as poor wages, bad working conditions, and unfair dismissal. Yet as members of individual groups with minority status, the rights of many of these individuals are often dictated by other types of law, such as constitutional and immigration laws.

The Civilian Conservation Corps

Formed in March 1933, the Civilian Conservation Corps, CCC, was one of the first New Deal programs. It was a public works project intended to promote environmental conservation and to build good citizens through vigorous, disciplined outdoor labor.

Sit-Down Strike

At 8 p.m. on December 30, 1936, in one of the first sit-down strikes in the United States, autoworkers occupy the General Motors Fisher Body Plant Number One in Flint, Michigan. The autoworkers were striking to win recognition of the United Auto Workers (UAW) as the only bargaining agent for GM's workers; they also wanted to make the company stop sending work to non-union plants and to establish a fair minimum wage scale, a grievance system and a set of procedures that would help protect assembly-line workers from injury. In all, the strike lasted 44 days.

The First 100 Days

Between 8 March and 16 June, in what later became known as the "First Hundred Days," Congress followed Roosevelt's lead by passing an incredible fifteen separate bills which, together, formed the basis of the New Deal. Several of the programs created during those three and a half months are still around in the federal government today.

National Industrial Recovery Act of 1933

The National Industrial Recovery Act of 1933 (NIRA) was one of the most important and daring measures of President Franklin D. Roosevelt's New Deal. It was enacted during the famous First Hundred Days of Roosevelt's first term in office and was the centerpiece of his initial efforts to reverse the economic collapse of the Great Depression. NIRA was signed into law on June 16, 1933, and was to remain in effect for two years. It attempted to make structural changes in the industrial sector of the economy and to alleviate unemployment with a public works program. It succeeded only partially in accomplishing its goals, and on May 27, 1935, less than three weeks before the act would have expired, the U.S. Supreme Court ruled it unconstitutional.

The Second New Deal

Despite the best efforts of President Roosevelt and his cabinet, however, the Great

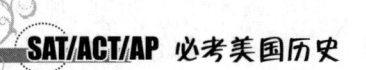

Depression continued—the nation's economy continued to wheeze; unemployment persisted; and people grew angrier and more desperate. So, in the spring of 1935, Roosevelt launched a second, more aggressive series of federal programs, sometimes called the Second New Deal. In April, he created the Works Progress Administration (WPA) to provide jobs for unemployed people.

Activating

1. Diagram

Draw a diagram to show the causes and the consequences of Great Depression.

2. Debate

Have a debate as the perspectives of Hoover and Hoover's wife.

Exercising

✍ Write an essay on the influence of New Deal. Dividing the influences into several parts like political influence, social influence, economic influence and so on will help you organize the essay more logically.

Great Depression and New Deal — Unit Seventeen

Homework

- ✎ Please group with another girl or boy. You and your partner need to prepare an elective speech as FDR and FDR's wife. In 20th century, Roosevelt's wife actually afforded to help Roosevelt's political career.
- ✎ Make a speech to compare and contrast the historic financial crisis in the world. The crisis's causes, results, influences and the solutions should be concerned.
- ✎ Think and discuss with the class whether the Second New Deal would pass or not and the reasons of your opinions. Your team needs to present your ideas.

Unit Eighteen

World War II—From Isolation to Intervention

1939	Cash-and-Carry Policy
	Nazi-Soviet Pact
	The movie *Mr. Smith Goes to Washington* was released
	John Steinbeck wrote *The Grapes of Wrath*
1940	Selective Service Act
	Tripartite Pact
	Roosevelt was elected to unprecedented third term
1941	Lend-Lease Act
	Japanese attack on Pearl Harbor
1942	Battle of Midway
1943	Teheran Conference
1944	Korematsu v. United States
	Bretton Woods Conference
1945	Battles of Iwo Jima and Okinawa
	Yalta Conference
	Potsdam Conference
	Dropping of the atomic bomb on Hiroshima and Nagasaki

Warming Up

1. Now that you've learned the lesson about the Great Depression and the New Deal, try predicting what would happen next. Would the world remain peaceful or would another war unfold?
2. After the nations involved in WWI signed the Treaty of Versailles, a French general said, "The treaty only brings us twenty years of peace." His view was proven correct. Is there any hint or prediction that another world war is in the cards later?

Historical Highlights

Facing WWII

Isolationism

Despite the United States participation in World War I and Wilson's international efforts to establish a new, peaceful global order, non-interventionist tendencies of US foreign policy were in full force in the aftermath of the war. The Senate rejected the Treaty of Versailles, which automatically rejected the United States' membership in the League of Nations. Non-interventionism or isolationism took a new turn during the Great Depression. President Herbert Hoover repeated the United States' commitment to isolationism while his successor,

Democrat Franklin Delano Roosevelt, translated this commitment into a number of foreign policy decisions, including the introduction of Good Neighbor Policy in Latin America. The policy aimed to replace earlier military interventions of the United States in Latin America with the principle of non-intervention and non-interference in the domestic affairs of Latin America.

Dangerous World Conditions

The United States existed in an increasingly dangerous world in the 1930s, creating new debates around the isolationist stance that had shaped foreign policy in the 1920s. The Fascist Party, led by Benito Mussolini, had taken power in Italy in 1922. The Nazi Party, led by Adolf Hitler, came to power in Germany in 1933. A civil war in Spain led to the rise of a government run by the dictator Francisco Franco in 1939. In Japan, militaristic leaders set Japan on an aggressive course. These dictatorial governments all took aggressive actions in the 1930s. Japan attacked China in 1931. Germany occupied the demilitarized Rhineland in 1936, annexed Austria in 1937, and occupied Czechoslovakia in 1939. Italy conquered Ethiopia in 1936. The League of Nations protested and Great Britain and France objected, but it was not until Germany attacked Poland in September 1939, that Hitler was seriously challenged. Great Britain and France declared war on Germany, beginning World War II. Germany, Italy, and Japan formed the Axis Powers with the signing of the Tripartite Pact (1940).

Argument for Intervention

While the U.S. Congress passed a number of so-called neutrality acts in the 1930s, fascism in Europe gained massive influence and the continent was on the brink of war. When in 1939 Germany invaded Poland, marking the outbreak of World War II, Americans were divided over the question of non-interventionism. The basic principle of the interventionist argument was fear of German invasion. By the summer of 1940, France suffered a stunning defeat by Germans, and Britain was the only democratic enemy of Germany. In a 1940 speech, Roosevelt argued, "Some, indeed, still hold to the now somewhat obvious delusion that we ... can safely permit the United States to become a lone island ... in a world dominated by the philosophy of force."

However, there were still many who held on to non-interventionism. Although a minority, they were well-organized, and had a powerful presence in Congress. Ultimately, the ideological rift between the ideals of the United States and the goals of the fascist powers empowered the interventionist argument. In 1941, the actions of the Roosevelt administration made it more and more clear that the United States was on a course to war.

Onset of World War II

Cash-and-Carry Policy

Cash and carry was a policy requested by U.S. President Franklin Delano Roosevelt. It replaced the Neutrality Acts of 1939. The revision allowed the sale of materiel to belligerents, as long as the recipients arranged for the transport using their own ships and paid immediately in cash, assuming all risk in transportation. Cash-and-carry policy was not going to be an effective measure after Germany began invading its neighbors. But it paved the way for Lend-Lease.

Attack on Pearl Harbor

Facing the problem of insufficient natural resources and following the ambition to become a major global power, the Japanese Empire began aggressive expansion in the 1930s. The American counter-proposal of November 26 required Japan to evacuate all of China without conditions and conclude non-aggression pacts with Pacific powers. However the day before the proposal was delivered (November 27 in Japan), on November 26 in Japan, the main Japanese attack fleet left port for Pearl Harbor. The attack came as a profound shock to the American people and led directly to the American entry into World War II in both the Pacific and European theaters. The following day (December 8), the United States declared war on Japan. Domestic support for non-interventionism, which had been traditionally strong and fading since the fall of France in 1940, disappeared.

United States at War

Entry into the European Theater

The United States entered the war in the west with Operation Torch in North Africa on 8 November 1942 although in mid-1942, the U.S. Army Air Forces (USAAF) arrived in the U.K. and carried out a few raids across the English Channel. In 1943, the U.S. participated in the Allies' invasion of Sicily and Italy. In July, the American seaborne assault landed on the southern coast of Sicily and units of an airborne division parachuted ahead of landings. On August 11, seeing that the battle was lost, the German and Italian commanders began evacuating their forces from Sicily to Italy. On 17 August, the Allies were in control of the island.

The first Allied troops landed on the Italian peninsula on 3 September 1943 and Italy surrendered on September 8 (although Mussolini's Italian Social Republic was established soon afterwards). The first American troops landed at Salerno on September 9, 1943. The Germans launched fierce counterattacks. The US 5th Army and other Allied armies broke through two German defensive lines (Volturno and the Barbara Line) in October and November 1943. After heavy winter and challenges that it posed to the Allies, Rome fell on June 4, 1944. Following the Normandy invasion in June 1944, the equivalent of seven US and French divisions were pulled out of Italy to participate in Operation Dragoon: the allied landings in southern France. Despite this the remaining US forces in Italy with other Allied forces pushed up to the last major defensive line in Northern Italy. The Italian Campaign ended on May 2, 1945 and US forces in mainland Italy suffered between 114,000 and over 119,000 casualties.

From 1942, numerous bombing runs were launched by the United States aimed at the industrial heart of Germany. In January 1943, at the Casablanca Conference, it was agreed Royal Air Force (RAF) Bomber Command operations against Germany would be reinforced by the USAAF in a Combined Operations Offensive plan called Operation Pointblank. At the beginning of the combined strategic bombing offensive on 4 March 1943, 669 RAF and 303 USAAF heavy bombers were available.

In the later stage of the war, the United States was heavily involved in the Operation Overlord (the code name for the Battle of Normandy)—the Allied operation that launched the successful invasion of German-occupied Western Europe. It commenced on June 6, 1944 with the Normandy landings (Operation Neptune, commonly known as D-Day). General Dwight D. Eisenhower was appointed commander of Supreme Headquarters Allied Expeditionary Force (SHAEF), and British General Bernard Montgomery was named as commander of the 21st Army Group, which comprised all the land forces involved in the invasion. In the months leading up to the invasion, the Allies conducted a substantial military deception, Operation Bodyguard, using both electronic and visual misinformation. This misled the Germans as to the date and location of the main Allied landings.

The Holocaust

The Holocaust, also known as the Shoah, was a genocide in which Adolf Hitler's Nazi Germany and its collaborators killed about six million Jews during World War II. The victims represented about two-thirds of the nine million Jews who had resided in Europe. Killings took place throughout Nazi Germany and German-occupied territories, with Nazi-occupied Poland constituting the geographical hub of the genocide. Out of eight Nazi extermination (or death) camps, designed to systematically kill millions, primarily by gassing, but also in mass executions and through extreme work under starvation conditions, six were built on the occupied Polish territory. The Nazis used the phrase "Final Solution to the Jewish Question" and the formula "Final Solution" has been widely used as a term for the genocide of the Jews.

US Involvement in the Pacific

The Battle of the Coral Sea

The Battle of the Coral Sea, May 4—8, 1942, was a major naval battle in the Pacific Theater of World War II between the Imperial Japanese Navy and Allied naval and air forces from the United States and Australia. The battle was the first action in which aircraft carriers engaged each other, as well as the first in which neither side's ships sighted or fired directly upon the other.

In an attempt to defend their empire in the South Pacific, Imperial Japanese forces decided to invade and occupy Port Moresby in New Guinea and Tulagi in the southeastern Solomon Islands. The plan to accomplish this, called Operation MO, involved several major units of Japan's Combined Fleet. The U.S. learned of the Japanese plan through signals intelligence and sent two United States Navy carrier task forces and a joint Australian-American cruiser force to oppose the Japanese offensive.

The Battle of Midway

The Battle of Midway was a decisive naval battle in the Pacific Theater of World War II. Between June 4 and 7, 1942, six months after Japan's attack on Pearl Harbor and one month after the Battle of the Coral Sea, the United States Navy decisively deflected an Imperial Japanese Navy attack against Midway Atoll, inflicting irreparable damage on the Japanese fleet.

War at Home

Demands imposed by the U.S. participation in World War II turned out to be the most effective measure to battle the long-lasting consequences of the Great Depression. The Roosevelt administration followed its New Deal approach and aimed to maintain significant control over the economy although many in the private industry resisted the idea. Government programs continued to recruit workers but this time the demand was fueled not by the economic crisis but by massive war demands. Production sped up dramatically, closed factories reopened and new ones were established creating millions of jobs in both private and public sectors, and many industries adjusted to the nearly insatiable needs of the military. Two-thirds of the American economy had been integrated into the war effort by the end of 1943.

Following the New Deal practice, the Roosevelt Administration established a number of new government agencies or expanded the role of those launched under the New Deal in order to convert the peacetime economy to the requirements imposed by the war effort. The Reconstruction Finance Corporation (RFC), originally established to provide loans to businesses, was now in control of eight wartime subsidiaries responsible for the management of critical natural resources and the production of synthetic alternatives at the time of constantly scarce supplies. The Office of Production Management (OPM) and the Supply Priorities and Allocations Board were both in charge of how natural resources were used for the war effort. The Office of Price Administration (OPA) was established within the Office for Emergency Management on August 28, 1941 to control prices (and thus inflation) and rents after the outbreak of World War II.

War Production

The most powerful of all war-time organizations whose task was to control the economy was the War Production Board (WPB), established by Roosevelt on January 16, 1942 by executive order. Its purpose was to regulate the production of materials during World War II in the United States. The WPB converted and expanded peacetime industries to meet war needs, allocated scarce materials vital to war production, established priorities in the distribution of materials and services, and prohibited nonessential production. It rationed such commodities as gasoline, heating oil, metals, rubber, paper, and plastics.

Labor

Because of the unprecedented labor demands, groups that were historically excluded from the labor market, particularly African Americans and women, received access to jobs. However, even the existing circumstances did not end discrimination, especially against the workers of color.

Shaping the Post-War World

Tehran Conference

The Tehran Conference was a strategy meeting of Joseph Stalin, Franklin D. Roosevelt, and Winston Churchill from 28 November to 1 December 1943. Although the three leaders arrived with differing objectives, the main outcome of the Tehran Conference was the Western Allies' commitment to open a second front against Nazi Germany. The conference also addressed the Allies' relations with Turkey and Iran, operations in Yugoslavia and against Japan, and the envisaged post-war settlement. A separate protocol signed at the conference pledged the Big Three to recognize Iran's independence.

Bretton Woods Conference

The Bretton Woods Conference was the gathering of 730 delegates from all 44 Allied nations at the Mount Washington Hotel, situated in Bretton Woods to regulate the international monetary and financial order after the conclusion of World War II.

After legislative ratification by member governments, agreements were signed to establish the International Bank for Reconstruction and Development (IBRD) and the International Monetary Fund (IMF).

Yalta Conference

The Yalta Conference, held from February 4 to 11, 1945, was the World War II meeting of the heads of government of the United States, the United Kingdom and the Soviet Union, represented by President Franklin D. Roosevelt, Prime Minister Winston Churchill and Premier Joseph Stalin, respectively, for the purpose of discussing Europe's post-war reorganization. The conference convened in the Livadia Palace near Yalta in Crimea.

The meeting was intended mainly to discuss the re-establishment of the nations of war-torn Europe. Within a few years, with the Cold War dividing the continent, Yalta became a subject of intense controversy. To a degree, it has remained controversial.

Potsdam Conference

The Potsdam Conference was held at Cecilienhof, Potsdam, occupied Germany, from 17 July to 2 August 1945. Participants were the Soviet Union, the United Kingdom and the United States. The three powers were represented by Communist Party General Secretary Joseph Stalin, Prime Ministers Winston Churchill and, later, Clement Attlee, and President Harry S. Truman.

Stalin, Churchill, and Truman—as well as Attlee gathered to decide how to administer the defeated Nazi Germany, which had agreed to unconditional surrender nine weeks earlier, on 8 May (V-E Day). The goals of the conference also included the establishment of post-war order, peace treaty issues, and countering the effects of the war.

End of World War II

The Atomic Bomb and the Defeat of Japan

On August 6, 1945, the U.S. dropped a uranium gun-type atomic bomb (Little Boy) on the city of Hiroshima. American President Harry S. Truman called for Japan's surrender 16 hours later, warning them to "expect a rain of ruin from the air, the like of which has never been seen on this earth." Three days later, on August 9, the U.S. dropped a plutonium implosion-type bomb (Fat Man) on the city of Nagasaki.

After several more days of behind-the-scenes negotiations and a failed coup d'état, Emperor Hirohito gave a recorded radio address across the Empire on August 15. In the radio address, he announced the surrender of Japan to the Allies.

V-E Day

Hitler made a last attempt to stop the Allied assault in the winter of 1944—1945. German forces drove through Allied lines into Belgium in the Battle of the Bulge before being stopped by Allied forces. American and British troops approached Germany from the west as Soviet troops approached from the east. By April 1945, Soviet troops were on the outskirts of Berlin. On April 30, Hitler committed suicide, and on May 7, 1945, Germany surrendered, ending the war in Europe.

Activating

Speech

After British Prime Minister Chamberlain represented Britain and signed policy of appeasement with Germany in 1930s, he said, "I believe it is peace for our time." At the time, he and other British citizens believed there was never going to be another world war. But they turned out to be wrong. Make a speech on the inevitability of World War II.

Exercising

✎ Essay: How do several international conferences establish the post-war world condition?

_____

_____
_____
_____
_____
_____
_____
_____

✎ Evaluate the reasons behind America's change from isolation to intervention during World War II.

_____

_____
_____
_____
_____
_____
_____
_____
_____

Homework

✎ Suppose during the Great Depression, Hitler and Franklin Roosevelt encountered an accident. As a result, their soul swapped. In another word, Hitler's soul rested in Franklin's body and Franklin Hitler's. Could America still walk out of the mire of Great Depression? Would America be another Germany in history? Or, are there other possibilities? Try imagining what changes would take place in history.

✎ Draw a map of post-war world conditions. Use different animals to mark the dominator of a certain area. (You can refer to the negotiations in several international conferences.)

World War II—From Isolation to Intervention Unit Eighteen

✍ Suppose you were the leader of one of the four nations below—America, Britain, China and Soviet Union. There would be another international conference following the three important meetings mentioned above. Give an address on the national benefits and requirements based on the world conditions.

Unit Nineteen

Cold War and Domestic Society

1944	G.I. Bill was passed
1946	*Baby and Child Care* by Dr. Benjamin Spock was published
	Largest strike wave in United States history
1947	Publication of the "X Article" ("The Sources of Soviet Conduct") by George Kennan
	Truman Doctrine (containment) was announced
	$400 million in military aid to Greece and Turkey
	House Un-American Affairs Committee began investigations of Hollywood
	Taft-Hartley Act
1948	Beginning of the Berlin Blockade
	President Truman issued order desegregating the military
	President Truman won election
1949	Formation of North Atlantic Treaty Organization (NATO)
1950	Senator Joseph McCarthy gained public spotlight on the issue of McCarthyism
	NSC-68 was adopted
	Beginning of Korean War

	Passage of McCarran Internal Security Act
1951	Truman fired General Douglas MacArthur
1952	United States tested world's first hydrogen bomb
	Dwight D. Eisenhower won presidential election
1953	Execution of Julius and Ethel Rosenberg
1954	Army—McCarthy hearings
	Brown v. Board of Education of Topeka
1955	Creation of Warsaw Pact
	Rosa Parks was arrested for not giving up her seat
1956	Interstate Highway Act
	Montgomery Bus Boycott
	Reelection of Eisenhower
1957	Soviet launch of the Sputnik satellite
	Founding of the Southern Christian Leadership Conference
	Crisis in Little Rock, Arkansas, over school desegregation
	On the Road by Jack Kerouac was published
1960	Soviet Union shot down U-2 spy plane
	Lunch-counter sit-in movement began
	Founding of the Student Non-Violent Coordinating Committee
1961	Bay of Pigs invasion in Cuba
1961	The Freedom Rides began
1962	Cuban Missile Crisis

Cold War and Domestic Society — Unit Nineteen

1963	Campaign to desegregate Birmingham, Alabama
	Assassination of President John F. Kennedy
	March on Washington, DC
	Martin Luther King, Jr., delivered his "I Have a Dream" speech
1964	Civil Rights Acts was passed
	"Freedom Summer" voter registration drive in Mississippi
	Killing of Michael Schwerner, James Chaney, and Andrew Goodman
	Gulf of Tonkin Resolution
1965	Voting Rights Act
	Malcolm X was assassinated
	March from Selma, Alabama, to Montgomery, Alabama
1966	Founding of the Black Panthers
1967	"Summer of Love"
	Rioting in Detroit, Newark, and other cities
1968	Assassination of Martin Luther King, Jr.
	Assassination of Robert F. Kennedy
	Violence at the Democratic Convention in Chicago
	Election of Richard Nixon
	Founding of the American Indian movement
1969	Woodstock Festival
	Stonewall Riot in New York City
	Apollo 11 landed on the moon

Warming Up

1. Suppose you were one of the following people: a woman, a returning white veteran, an African American, or a farmer. What kind of changes would you face following WW II?
2. Compare the famous quotes from Adam Smith and Karl Marx who respectively are ancestors of capitalism and communism. Is there some conflict underlying? Can the two ideologies exist at the same time?

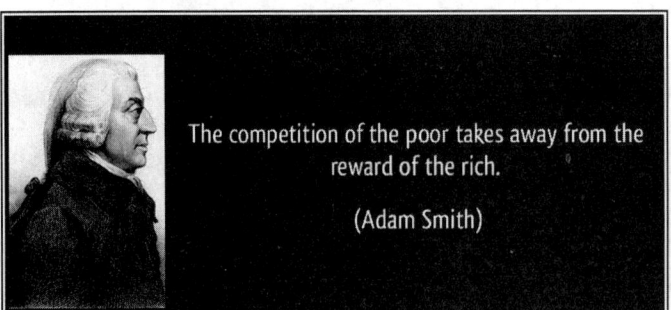

The competition of the poor takes away from the reward of the rich.

(Adam Smith)

THE RICH WILL DO ANYTHING FOR THE POOR BUT GET OFF THEIR BACKS.

Karl Marx
Prussian-German philosopher
(1818-1883)

It is not by augmenting the capital of the country, but by rendering a greater part of that capital active and productive than would otherwise be so, that the most judicious operations of banking can increase the industry of the country.

—Adam Smith

It is not from the benevolence of the butcher, the brewer, or the baker that we expect our dinner, but from their regard to their own interest.

—Adam Smith

Let the ruling classes tremble at a communist revolution. The proletarians have nothing to lose but their chains. They have a world to win. Workingmen of all countries, unite!

—Karl Marx

Capital is dead labor, which, vampire-like, lives only by sucking living labor, and lives the more, the more labor it sucks.

—Karl Marx

Cold War and Domestic Society — Unit Nineteen

Historical Highlights

Origins of the Cold War

The Origins of the Cold War are widely regarded to lie most directly in the relations between the Soviet Union and the Allies (the United States, Great Britain and France) in the years 1945—1947. Those events led to the Cold War that endured for just under half a century.

Events preceding the Second World War, and even the Russian Revolution of 1917, underlay pre-World War II tensions between the Soviet Union, western European countries and the United States. A series of events during and after World War II exacerbated tensions, including the Soviet-German pact during the first two years of the war leading to subsequent invasions, the perceived delay of an amphibious invasion of German-occupied Europe, the western allies' support of the Atlantic Charter, disagreement in wartime conferences over the fate of Eastern Europe, the Soviets' creation of an Eastern Bloc of Soviet satellite states, western allies scrapping the Morgenthau Plan to support the rebuilding of German industry, and the Marshall Plan.

Tensions Grow

In February 1946, U.S. diplomat George F. Kennan delivered a memo from his post in Moscow which came to be known as the Long Telegram. The Long Telegram sought to explain recent Soviet behavior to Kennan's superiors in Washington, and further advised a hard line against the Soviets. It argued that the Soviet Union was motivated by both traditional Russian imperialism and by Marxist ideology, which advocated the expansion of socialism, the transition to communism, and the toppling of capitalist regimes. In Kennan's view, Soviet behavior was inherently expansionist and paranoid, posing a threat to the United States and its allies.

That September, the Soviets produced the Novikov Telegram. This telegram, sent by the Soviet ambassador to the US, portrayed the US as being in the grip of monopolistic capitalists bent on building up military capability "to prepare the conditions for winning world supremacy in a new war." These differing interpretations of international politics in the immediate postwar era set the stage for a succession of diplomatic, economic, and military confrontations between the two powers.

Policies of Containment

Containment was a U.S. policy that used numerous strategies to prevent the spread of communism abroad. A component of the Cold War, this policy was a response to a series of moves by the Soviet Union to enlarge communist influence in Eastern Europe, China, Korea, and Vietnam. It represented a middle-ground position between détente and rollback.

According to Kennan, the Soviet Union did not see the possibility for long-term peaceful coexistence with the capitalist world. It was its ever-present aim to advance the socialist cause. Capitalism was a menace to the ideals of socialism, and capitalists could not be trusted or allowed to influence the Soviet people. Outright conflict was never considered a desirable avenue for the propagation of the Soviet cause, but their eyes and ears were always open for the opportunity to take advantage of "diseased tissue" anywhere in the world.

Truman Doctrine

In March 1947, President Truman, a Democrat, asked the Republican-controlled Congress to appropriate $400 million in aid to the Greek and Turkish governments, then fighting Communist subversion. Truman pledged to "support free peoples who are resisting attempted subjugation by armed minorities or by outside pressures." This pledge became known as the Truman Doctrine. Portraying the issue as a mighty clash between "totalitarian regimes" and "free peoples," the speech marks the onset of the Cold War and the adoption of containment as official U.S. policy. Congress appropriated the money.

Truman followed up his speech with a series of measures to contain Soviet influence in Europe, including the Marshall Plan and NATO, a military alliance between the U.S. and Western European nations.

Because containment required detailed information about Communist moves, the government relied increasingly on the Central Intelligence Agency (CIA). Established by the National Security Act of 1947, the CIA conducted espionage in foreign lands, some of it visible, more of it secret. The Soviet Union's first nuclear test in 1949 prompted the National Security Council to formulate a revised security doctrine. Completed in April 1950, it became known as NSC 68. It concluded that a massive military build-up was necessary to the deal with the Soviet threat.

"Domino Theory"

The domino theory, which governed much of U.S. foreign policy beginning in the early 1950s, held that a communist victory in one nation would quickly lead to a chain reaction of communist takeovers in neighboring states. In Southeast Asia, the United States government used the domino theory to justify its support of a non-communist regime in South

Vietnam against the communist government of North Vietnam, and ultimately its increasing involvement in the long-running Vietnam War (1954—1975). In fact, the American failure to prevent a communist victory in Vietnam had much less of a global impact than had been assumed by the domino theory. Though communist regimes did arise in Laos and Cambodia after 1975, communism failed to spread throughout the rest of Southeast Asia.

The Marshall Plan

The Marshall Plan (officially the European Recovery Program) was an American initiative to aid Western Europe, in which the United States gave $13 billion in economic support to help rebuild Western European economies after the end of World War Ⅱ. The initiative was named after Secretary of State George Marshall. The Plan was largely the creation of State Department officials such as George F. Kennan. The plan was established on June 5, 1947, and was in operation for four years beginning in April 1948.

The Berlin Blockade

As part of the economic rebuilding of Germany, in early 1948, representatives of a number of Western European governments and the United States announced an agreement for a merger of western German areas into a federal governmental system. In addition, in accordance with the Marshall Plan, they began to re-industrialize and rebuild the German economy, including the introduction of a new Deutsche Mark currency to replace the old Reichsmark currency that the Soviets had debased.

Shortly thereafter, Stalin instituted the Berlin Blockade (24 June 1948—12 May 1949), one of the first major crises of the Cold War, preventing food, materials and supplies from arriving in West Berlin. The Soviet Union blocked the Western Allies' railway, road, and canal access to the sectors of Berlin under Western control. The Soviets offered to drop the blockade if the Western Allies withdrew the newly introduced Deutsche mark from West Berlin.

In response, the Western Allies organized the Berlin airlift to carry supplies to the people of West Berlin, a difficult feat given the city's population. The Soviets did not disrupt the airlift for fear this might lead to open conflict.

NATO

The North Atlantic Treaty Organization (NATO) is an intergovernmental military alliance based on the North Atlantic Treaty which was signed on April 4, 1949. The organization constitutes a system of collective defense whereby its member states agree to mutual defense in response to an attack by any external party.

Warsaw Pact

One of the immediate results of West Germany's integration into NATO was the creation of the Warsaw Pact, which was signed on 14 May 1955 by the Soviet Union, Hungary, Czechoslovakia, Poland, Bulgaria, Romania, Albania, and East Germany. The Warsaw Pact was a formal response to West Germany's integration, and clearly delineated the two opposing sides of the Cold War. While the Warsaw Pact was established as a balance of power or counterweight to NATO, there was no direct confrontation between them. Instead, the conflict was fought on an ideological basis. Both NATO and the Warsaw Pact led to the expansion of military forces and their integration into the respective blocs.

NSC-68

National Security Council Report 68 (NSC-68) was a 58-page top secret policy paper presented to President Harry S. Truman on April 14, 1950. It was one of the most important statements of American policy that launched the Cold War. In the words of scholar Ernest R. May, NSC-68 "provided the blueprint for the militarization of the Cold War from 1950 to the collapse of the Soviet Union at the beginning of the 1990s." NSC-68 and its subsequent amplifications advocated a large expansion in the military budget of the United States.

Domestic Social Conditions

Conservatism

McCarthyism and the Second Red Scare

McCarthyism is the practice of making accusations of disloyalty, subversion, or treason without proper regard for evidence. The term has its origins in the period in the United States known as the Second Red Scare, lasting roughly from 1950 to 1956 and characterized by heightened fears of communist influence on American institutions and espionage by Soviet agents. "McCarthyism" was originally coined to criticize the anti-communist pursuits of Republican U.S. Senator Joseph McCarthy of Wisconsin.

While Communism was expanding across Europe and Asia, the United States entered an era of paranoia known as the Red Scare. McCarthy used his position to make often sensational accusations of Communist infiltration into the State Department, the Democratic administration of President Harry S. Truman, and the United States Army. During that speech, he produced a piece of paper which he claimed contained a list of known Communists working for the State Department. McCarthy is usually quoted as saying: "I have here in my hand a list of 205—a list of names that were made known to the Secretary of State as being members of the Communist Party and who nevertheless are still working and shaping policy in the State Department." McCarthyism began to lose its potency as the perceived threat of Communism receded during the latter half of the 1950s.

The Threat of Nuclear War

Although the Soviet Union had nuclear weapon capabilities in the beginning of the Cold War, the United States still had an advantage in terms of bombers and weapons. In any exchange of hostilities, the United States would have been capable of bombing the Soviet Union, whereas the Soviet Union would have more difficulty carrying out the reverse mission. In 1960, the United States developed its first *Single Integrated Operational Plan*, a range of targeting options, and described launch procedures and target sets against which nuclear weapons would be launched, variants of which were in use from 1961 to 2003. That year also saw the start of the Missile Defense Alarm System, an American system of 12 early-warning satellites that provided limited notice of Soviet intercontinental ballistic missile launches. However, a complex and worrisome situation developed in 1962, in what is called the Cuban Missile Crisis.

The Rosenberg Case

Julius and Ethel Rosenberg were American citizens who spied for the Soviet Union and were tried, convicted, and executed for conspiracy to commit espionage. They were instrumental in the passing of information about the atomic bomb to the Soviet Union under Joseph Stalin, speeding his development of Soviet nuclear weapon. Other captured co-conspirators were imprisoned.

Smith Act and Communist

Smith Act is a United States federal statute that set criminal penalties for advocating the overthrow of the U.S. government and required all non-citizen adult residents to register with the government. During Cold War, many communists were arrested under the Act. Prosecutions under the Smith Act continued until a series of United States Supreme Court decisions in 1957 reversed a number of convictions under the Act as unconstitutional.

Sputnik

Soviet Union successfully launched Sputnik I in 1957, the world's first artificial satellite. That launch ushered in new political, military, technological, and scientific developments. While the Sputnik launch was a single event, it marked the start of the space age and the

U.S.-U.S.S.R space race. The Sputnik launch changed everything. As a technical achievement, Sputnik caught the world's attention and the American public off-guard. In addition, the public feared that the Soviets' ability to launch satellites also translated into the capability to launch ballistic missiles that could carry nuclear weapons from Europe to the U.S.

Korean War

Korean War was the first hot war of the Cold War: 1950—1953. During Second World War, the Allies decided to divide Korea at the 38th parallel. The North was under the trusteeship of the Soviet Union, the South under the trusteeship of the Americans. Two different countries developed: the North became a communist country, the South a non-communist, democratic country. Both sides wanted to re-unify the country under their own rule. In 1950, after a number of small skirmishes at the border, war broke out between North and South Korea. The US backed and fought with the South, and China backed and fought with the North. Initially, American and United Nations' forces pushed deep into North Korea; however, China entered the war and pushed the Americans backed into the South. After three years, the two sides fought to a stalemate and kept the country divided at the 38th parallel.

Modernity

Post-War Prosperity

The immediate years following World War II witnessed stability and prosperity for many Americans. Increasing numbers of workers enjoyed high wages, larger houses, better schools, more cars and home comforts like vacuum cleaners, washing machines—which were all made for labor-saving and to make housework easier. Inventions familiar in the early 21st century made their first appearance during this era. The American economy grew dramatically in the post-war period, expanding at a rate of 3.5% per annum between 1945 and 1970. Couples who could not afford families during the Great Depression made up for lost time; the mood was now optimistic. Such condition fostered baby boom. During this period, many incomes doubled in a generation. The new prosperity did not extend to everyone. Many Americans continued to live in poverty throughout the 1950s, especially older people and African Americans, the latter of whom continued to earn far less than their white counterparts on average in the two decades following the end of the Second World War.

The G.I. Bill

G.I. Bill was a law that provided a range of benefits for returning World War II veterans. Benefits included low-cost mortgages, low-interest loans to start a business, cash payments of tuition and living expenses to attend university, high school or vocational education, as well as one year of unemployment compensation. It was available to veterans who had been on active duty during the war years. Historians and economists judge the G.I. Bill a major political and economic success—especially in contrast to the treatments of World War I veterans—and a major contribution to America's stock of human capital that sped long-term economic growth.

Post-War Suburban Era

The suburban population in North America exploded during the post-World War II economic expansion. Returning veterans wishing to start a settled life moved in masses to the suburbs. Levittown developed as a major prototype of mass-produced housing. At the same time, African Americans were rapidly moving north for better jobs and educational opportunities than were available to them in the segregated South. Their arrival in Northern cities and hostility of many white Americans further stimulated white suburban migration. 1950 was the first year that more Americans lived in suburbs than elsewhere.

White Flight

With the growth of the suburbs in the early and mid-20th century, a pattern of hypersegregation—a form of racial segregation that consists of the geographical grouping of racial groups—emerged. In the early-20th century, African Americans who moved to large U.S. cities typically moved into the inner-city to gain industrial jobs. The influx of new black residents caused many white Americans to move to the suburbs ("white flight"). During the 1940s, for the first time a powerful interaction between segregation laws and race differences in terms of socioeconomic status enabled white families to abandon inner cities in favor of suburban living. The eventual result was severe levels of urban decay that, by the 1960s, resulted in the crumbling urban "ghettos."

Wave of Strikes

Throughout the Second World War, the National War Labor Board gave trade unions the responsibility for maintaining labor discipline in exchange for closed membership. This led to acquiescence on the part of labor leaders to businesses and various wildcat strikes on the part of the workers. Often the strikes were against work discipline. After the war, wages fell across the board, leading to large strikes. In 1947, Congress responded to the strike wave by passing, over President Truman's veto, the Taft-Hartley Act, restricting the powers and activities of labor unions. The act is still in force as of 2016.

The Interstate Highway Act

National Interstate and Defense Highways Act was enacted in 1956, when President Dwight D. Eisenhower signed the bill into law. With an original authorization of US$25 billion for the construction of 41,000 miles of the Interstate Highway System supposedly over a 10-year period, it was the largest public works project in American history through that time. The addition of the term "defense" in the act's title was for two reasons: First, some of the original cost was diverted from defense funds. Secondly, most U.S. Air Force bases have a direct link to the system. The purpose was to provide access in order to defend them during an attack.

Civil Rights Movement

African Americans returned from WW II with a sense of self-pride, only to meet with the rooted spite. Civil Rights Movement encompasses social movements in the United States whose goals were to end racial segregation and discrimination against African Americans and to secure legal recognition and federal protection of the citizenship rights enumerated in the Constitution and federal law. While black Americans had been fighting for their rights and liberties since the time of slavery, the 1950s and 1960s witnessed critical accomplishments in their civil rights struggle.

Civil Resistance

The movement was characterized by major campaigns of civil resistance. Between 1955 and 1968, acts of nonviolent protest and civil disobedience produced crisis situations between activists and government authorities. Federal, state, and local governments, businesses, and communities often had to respond immediately to these situations that highlighted the discrimination faced by African Americans. Forms of protest or civil disobedience included boycotts such as the successful Montgomery Bus Boycott in Alabama; "sit-ins" such as the influential Greensboro sit-ins; marches, such as the Selma to Montgomery marches in Alabama or the march on Washington as well as a wide range of other nonviolent activities.

Brown v. Board of Education

A critical Supreme Court decision of this phase of the Civil Rights Movement was the 1954 Brown v. Board of Education. In the spring of 1951, black students in Virginia protested their unequal status in the state's segregated educational system. Students at Moton High School protested the overcrowded conditions and failing facility. Some local leaders of the NAACP had tried to persuade the students to back down from their protest against the Jim Crow laws of school segregation. When the students did not budge, the NAACP joined their battle against school segregation. The NAACP proceeded with five cases challenging the school systems; these were later combined under what is known today as Brown v. Board of Education.

In 1954, the U.S. Supreme Court ruled unanimously that mandating, or even permitting, public schools to be segregated by race was unconstitutional. However, the new law raised controversy. As late as 1957, three years after the decision, a crisis erupted in Little Rock, Arkansas when Governor of Arkansas Orval Faubus called out the National Guard on September 4 to prevent entry to the nine African-American students who had sued for the right to attend an integrated school, Little Rock Central High School. The nine students had been chosen to attend Central High because of their excellent grades. Faubus' resistance received the attention of President Dwight D. Eisenhower, who was determined to enforce the orders of the Federal courts. Critics had charged he was lukewarm, at best, on the goal of desegregation of public schools. However, Eisenhower federalized the National Guard in Arkansas and ordered them to return to their barracks. He deployed elements of the 101st Airborne Division to Little Rock to protect the students.

The Montgomery Bus Boycott

The Montgomery bus boycott was a political and social protest campaign against the policy of racial segregation on the public transit system of Montgomery, Alabama. The campaign lasted from December 5, 1955—when Rosa Parks, an African American woman, was arrested for refusing to surrender her seat to a white person—to December 20, 1956, when a federal ruling, Browder v. Gayle, took effect, and led to a United States Supreme Court decision that declared the Alabama and Montgomery laws requiring segregated buses to be unconstitutional. Many important figures in the Civil Rights Movement took part in the boycott, including Reverend Martin Luther King, Jr. and Ralph Abernathy.

Martin Luther King, Jr.

Martin Luther King, Jr. was an American clergyman, activist, and prominent leader in the African-American Civil Rights Movement. He is best known for his practice of nonviolent civil disobedience based on his Christian beliefs. Later in his career, King's message highlighted more radical social justice questions, which alienated many of his liberal allies.

Post-War Culture

Conformity

The end of one war and the beginnings of the Cold War created real stresses in American social life. Soldiers returned from the war eager to return to normal life, to buy homes, start families, and hold regular jobs. There was a national enthusiasm for a return to normality that created pressures for people to conform to standards of behavior. Also, the existence of communism and McCarthyism made many Americans feel intimidated to be nonconformist. Gradually, a conservative life pattern was recommended.

Red Scare

As the Cold War between the Soviet Union and the United States intensified in the late 1940s and early 1950s, hysteria over the perceived threat posed by Communists in the U.S. became known as the Red Scare. (Communists were often referred to as "Reds" for their allegiance to the red Soviet flag.) The Red Scare led to a range of actions that had a profound and enduring effect on U.S. government and society. Federal employees were analyzed to determine whether they were sufficiently loyal to the government, and the House Un-American Activities Committee, as well as U.S. Senator Joseph R. McCarthy, investigated allegations of subversive elements in the government and the Hollywood film industry. The climate of fear and repression linked to the Red Scare finally began to ease by the late 1950s.

Television

After World War II, American homes were invaded by a powerful new force— television. The idea of seeing "live" shows in the living room was immediately attractive. The effects of this powerful medium are still being measured. Television has developed since World War II into the most popular medium in the United States, one that has had great influence on American way of life. Virtually every American household—98% in 1999—has at least one TV set.

Rock and Roll Music

Rock and roll is a genre of popular music that originated and evolved in the United States during the late 1940s and early 1950s, from combined African-American and European American rooted genres known as gospel music, blues, boogie-woogie, jump blues, jazz, etc. Rock and roll have contributed to the civil rights movement because both African-American and white American teens enjoyed the music. Passionate genre of Rock and Roll Music also helped express feelings of the African Americans. The migration of many former slaves and their descendants to major urban centers such as Memphis, New York City, Detroit, Chicago, Cleveland, and Buffalo meant that black and white residents were living in close proximity in larger numbers than ever before, and as a result heard each other's music and even began to emulate each other's fashions.

Beat Generation Literature

The Beat Generation was a group of authors whose literature explored and influenced American culture in the post-World War II era. Feeling the devastation of WW II, Americans got tired of the standard life as well as the so-called democracy. Eager for a special way for release, a group of American authors inaugurated a new literature theme. Beat Generation thus also mirrored the spiritual condition of contemporary Americans. The bulk of their work was published and popularized throughout the 1950s. Central elements of Beat culture were rejection of standard narrative values, the spiritual quest, exploration of American and Eastern religions, rejection of materialism, explicit portrayals of the human condition, experimentation with psychedelic drugs, and sexual liberation and exploration.

Activating

1. Speech

Martin Luther King's world-famous speech *I Have A Dream* is full of eloquence and passion. Please take the speech as a model and make your own one on the rights of African Americans. Express how you feel and what you want as an African American.

2. Debate

During the Cold War, both America and Soviet Union provided economic and military aid to European and Asian nations. Meanwhile, the United Nations and several international authorities sprang up. Some experts believed that hidden by the bi-polar world condition is the multi-polar trend in future. However, others argued that it was the establishment of these international authorities that reduced the power of every nation involved. Is Cold War the disaster of superpower conflicts or the cradle for future multi-polar balance?

Exercising

✎ Complete the chart below on Cold War.

	Name of Cold War Policy	Brief Introduction
America		
Soviet Union		

✎ Assess the effects of Cold War from two perspectives: international influence, domestic (American) influence.

_____

_____

_____

_____

_____

_____

_____

_____

Homework

✎ Search more information on Rock 'n' Roll music. Try creating some Rock 'n' Roll music (including lyrics and tune). If some students have mastery over music, they can form a team and perform the show!

✎ Beat Generation delegates another brand-new way to cope with the post-war world excerpt

sticking to conformity. Create some beat generation literature; it should show the feature of the era. Genre unlimited (novel, poem, song, drama…).

✎ Choose a certain period during Cold War or even a detailed date in between. Make a whole set of newspaper at the time.

Tips: You can search information about the journalism characteristics, diction feature, political cartoon at the time.

Unit Twenty

Modern Politics

Warming Up

1. During the 2016 presidential election, how did you feel about the idea of democracy? Why did the "crazy, anti-democratic" Trump have a chance to win?
   (Clinton/Trump)
2. Have you seen *House of Cards*? What's your opinion about politics?

Historical Highlights

The Presidency of John. F. Kennedy

The New Frontier

JFK aimed to make changes in Social Security benefits as well as deal with poverty and racial discrimination. Several representative acts are the Vocational Educational Act which provides funds to expand vocational training and the Area Redevelopment Act which gave funds to industries willing to build in depressed area. Kennedy also promoted deficit spending to stimulate the economy.

The Peace Corps (1961)

Kennedy established the Peace Corps in 1961. The Peace Corps is a program which sends volunteers from the US to assist underdeveloped countries worldwide.

The Assassination of Kennedy

On November 22, 1963, President Kennedy was assassinated by Lee Harvey Oswald while visiting Dallas, Texas. This assassination shocked the whole nation.

The Presidency of Lyndon B. Johnson

The Great Society

The aim of the great society was to put an end to poverty and racial discrimination, and create opportunities for every child. The Economic Opportunity Act in 1964 included preparing underprivileged children for school, helping the poor to go to university, getting volunteer skills to help the poor, creating a Model Cities Program and giving training to high school drop-outs.

Social Welfare

Johnson also tackled health care, Johnson created Medicare, hospital insurance for Americans in the Social Security System who were age 65 or older. He also pushed for improved educational conditions, including improving school libraries. Moreover, he prompted two acts—The Water Quality Act (1965) and the Clean Water Restoration Act (1966).

The Warren Court

The Warren Court was the Supreme Court of the 1960s under Chief Justice Earl Warren and promoted civil rights. It protected the rights of minorities, reinforced the separation of church and state, established the individual rights of privacy and protected the rights of people accused of crimes.

The Vietnam War

The Vietnam War between communist-controlled North Vietnam and western-allied South Vietnam officially began after Johnson announced that an American destroyer had been fired upon in the Gulf of Tonkin, prompting congress to declare war. The US sided with South Vietnam.

Foreign Policy

Johnson signed US-Soviet Nuclear Proliferation Treaty (1968) which set limits on nuclear weapon use. With Latin America, he ordered over 20,000 Marines to the Dominican Republic to help resist communism. Also notable is that he was president when Neil

Armstrong became the first man to set foot on the Moon during the Apollo Space Program that began under JFK.

Civil Rights Movement in the 1960s

The civil rights movement continued into the 1960s. In 1961, CORE organized a series of bus rides through the South to challenge segregation on interstate bus routes. In 1963, over 200,000 people gathered to march, sing, and hear Martin Luther King's speech "I have a dream" in Washington, D.C.

The Presidency of Richard M. Nixon

Foreign Policy

In 1968, Nixon won the election and became the president. During his presidency, he made significant progress in pursuing a policy of detente with China and the Soviet Union. In 1971, America and Soviet Union made an agreement that Soviet Union recognized the independence of West Berlin and America recognized East Germany. In 1972, The Strategic Arms Limitation Talks (SALT) led to the control of arms. The same year, Nixon visited China, which resulted in diplomatic exchange and the US recognition of China in 1979. However, with Vietnam, he began the policy of *Vietnamization* which widened the war.

Domestic Policy

In 1970, the Nixon administration created the Environment Protection Agency and passed the Clean Air Act and the Clean Water Act. As time progressed, the economy experienced both recession and inflation. In 1973, oil supplies faced serious crisis because of various conflicts in the middle east.

Civil Rights

As a "southern strategy," Nixon tried to place a number of conservative southerners as judges in federal courts. He nominated Clement Haynsworth and G. Harrold Carswell to serve on the court. Also, he initiated Philadelphia Plan which required labor unions and federal contractors to submit goals and timetables for hiring minorities.

The Watergate Scandal

Nixon's reelection campaign tried to place phone taps in the Democratic Party headquarters to record the conversations of political opponents. This event was known as the Watergate Scandal. As a result, Nixon forced to resign.

The Presidency of Gerald. R. Ford and James E. Carter

Ford Pardons Nixon and Economic Policy

Ford assumed the presidency after Nixon resigned. In 1974, Ford pardoned Richard Nixon for any crimes he might have committed as president. Ford's most well-known economic policy to fight inflation was the Whip Inflation Now (WIN) campaign. The campaign encouraged people to be more disciplined with their money. However, this act failed.

Carter's Leadership and Economic Inflation

From the beginning of Carter's presidency, he tried to portray himself as a citizen's president. But his inexperience gave him lots of trouble. Carter gave amnesty to Americans who had avoided the draft in the Vietnam War. Besides, he also needed to fight inflation and energy crisis. Carter called on Americans to conserve crude oil and also raised taxes on oil. The Federal Reserve Board's header—Paul Volcker, nominated by Carter, began to raise interest rates.

Foreign Policy (Relations with Soviet Union, Middle East)

Relations with the Soviet Union remained central to US foreign policy during Ford's and Carter's presidency. Under Ford's direction, United States continued disarmament talks with Soviets and made an agreement called SALT II which limited nuclear arm production. Carter withdrew the SALT II treaty from Senate consideration and imposed sanctions on the Soviets after the Soviet Union invaded Afghanistan in 1979. The relationship with Soviets thus cooled down. Carter also helped negotiate a historic peace agreement between Israel and Egypt.

The Presidency of Ronald Reagan

Domestic Policy of Reagan

Reagan won the presidential election in 1980 and clearly opposed what he considered to be big government. He also made clear his support for a strong military and belief in traditional values. Based on the conservative theory of "supply-side economics," he proposed and passed the Economic Recovery Act of 1981. In the act, taxes were reduced by 25 percent over three years and social spending was reduced. The government also deregulated the economy. Beginning in early 1983, the economy slowly began to turn around, but government budget deficits worsened.

Foreign Policy (Reagan Doctrine)

Reagan thought that the United States should seek to roll back Soviet rule in Eastern

Europe and elsewhere rather than détente. He wanted to challenge communism as much as possible without provoking war. So he built up the US military and aided anti-communists. Finally, the cold war came to an end and Soviet Union broke apart.

The Presidency of George Bush

Domestic Policy of Bush

George H.W. Bush won the presidency in 1988 and he promoted no more taxes to gain support. In fact, this promise didn't come true.

Foreign Policy (Persian Gulf War, The War on Drugs, South America—Democracy)

The most significant foreign act of Bush was the Persian Gulf War. On August 2, 1990, Iraq invaded its neighbor Kuwait. The Iraqi forces quickly overran the Kuwaitis. Responding to this situation, many countries sent troops and Congress allowed America to use force. Then, Operation Desert Storm, the name of the American led attack on Iraqi forces, began on September 1991. After the battle, Iraq agreed to sanctions, a no-fly zone, and a cease fire.

The Presidency of Bill Clinton

Domestic Policy

Early in his presidency, Clinton signed the Family Medical Leave Act which guaranteed most full time employees 12 workweeks of unpaid leave each year for many reasons. Clinton also wanted a program that would guarantee care for all Americans. He tried but ultimately failed. Clinton also tried to address the issue of violence in society. In 1993, he signed the Brady Bill on gun control.

Scandals, Impeachment and Trial

Presidents Clinton had two scandals during his presidency. One concerned investment was that Bill and Hillary Clinton had made in the Whitewater Development Corporation, a real estate company, in the 1970s and 1980s. Another was his relationship with a White House intern. The House of Representatives impeached Clinton on the charges of perjury and obstruction of justice. But after the vote of Senate, Clinton was acquitted.

Foreign Policy

In South Africa, Mandela was elected. In the Middle East, conflicts continued between

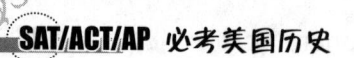

Israel and PLO. Also, NATO expanded because some countries joined.

The Presidency of George W. Bush

Domestic Policy

Like many republicans, Bush believed that tax cuts would stimulate the economy and create new jobs. In 2001, he pursued a highly controversial 1.3 trillion tax cut through Congress. Other domestic policy was education. In 2002, the No Child Left Behind Act penalized schools that did not meet federal school performance guidelines. He also promoted improvements in teacher quality and other educational reforms, but left the program underfunded.

War on Terror

On September 11, 2001, terrorists hijacked four commercial passenger airplanes and crashed two of them into the World Trade Center in New York City. After this attack, Bush agreed that the most important priority should be tracking down the people behind 9/11, primarily Osama Bin Laden. When the Taliban government refused to turn over Bin Laden, American forces invaded Afghanistan. Additionally, Congress passed Patriot Act to give law enforcement broader and sometimes questionable powers to monitor, investigate and detain suspected terrorists.

The Presidency of Barack Obama

Domestic Policy

President Obama developed an economic stimulus package which included tax cuts and funds for infrastructure projects to help economy. The 787 billion dollar bill was approved by Congress in February 2009. Obama also proposed and signed the Affordable Care Act, designed to allow healthcare options for all Americans.

Foreign Policy

In August 2010, Obama announced "The American combat mission in Iraq has ended." Iraq was significantly more stable, although terrorism still existed. In May 2011, President Obama announced the death of Bin Laden.

Modern Politics **Unit Twenty**

Activating

1. Debate

Does terrorism an inevitable trend as America progresses?

2. Imitation Speech

If you are a candidate running for president, how do you get your vote in the election? Be charismatic!

Exercising

✎ Write a passage to show your opinion on the following questions.

1) How do you think America deal with hegemonism and democracy?

2) Is "American democracy" real democracy?

_____

_____
_____
_____
_____
_____
_____
_____
_____
_____
_____
_____
_____

Homework

✎ Make a chart to show the 12 presidents of America and their historic events. Also, choose one to give a presentation.

(The 12 presidents are Harry S. Truman, Dwight D. Eisenhower, John F. Kennedy, Lyndon Johnson, Richard Nixon, Gerald Ford, Jimmy Carter, Ronald Reagan, George H. W. Bush, Bill Clinton, George W. Bush, Barack Obama.)

✎ Compare and contrast the political opinion of each president. Which one do you think is the best president ever?

✎ Create your own psychological test on whether a person is individualistic heroism or collectivism. You might find some other psychological tests to get some inspiration.

✎ Write a film script on one of the 6 topics.

1) The relationship between media and public opinion.

2) The relationship between the president and the country.

3) Terrorism.

4) The country under Barack Obama and the country without presidents.

5) Individualism VS. collectivism.

6) Hegemonism.

✎ Create a spider chart for each of 12 presidents to show their characteristics and abilities. Here is an example of a spider chart. You might have seen it in games.

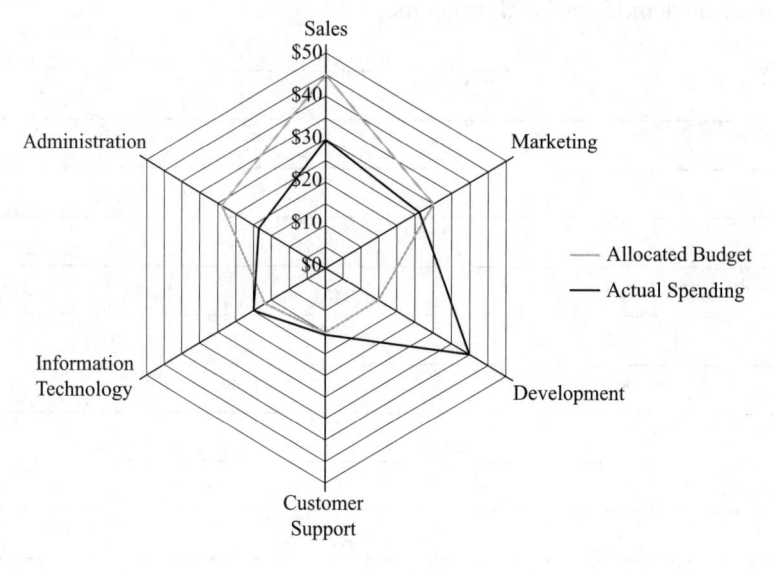